MASTERS'
JIU JITSU

MASTERS'

JIU JITSU

**An official book of the
Martial Arts Commission**

Robert Clark

PELHAM BOOKS

PELHAM BOOKS

Published by the Penguin Group
27 Wrights Lane, London W8 5TY, England
Viking Penguin Inc., 40 West 23rd Street,
New York, New York 10010, USA
Penguin Books Australia Ltd, Ringwood,
Victoria, Australia
Penguin Books Canada Ltd, 2801 John Street,
Markham, Ontario, Canada L3R 1B4
Penguin Books (NZ) Ltd, 182-190 Wairau
Road, Auckland 10, New Zealand

Penguin Books Ltd, Registered Offices:
Harmondsworth, Middlesex, England

First published in 1988

© 1988 The Bowerdean Press

'A CIP catalogue record for this book is
available from the British Library'

ISBN 0 7207 1845 7

Designed and produced by
The Bowerdean Press Ltd.
London EC1

Typeset by Chambers Wallace Ltd.,
London
Printed and bound in England by
Redwood Burn Ltd., Trowbridge,
Wiltshire

The Martial Arts are potentially
dangerous: the author, producers and
publishers will accept no liability for
damage or injuries resulting from the
performance of techniques described in
this book.

Contents

Introduction

The development of unarmed combat

As long as man has inhabited the earth, strife and warfare have been unending. Whether squabbling over access to a water hole, or disputing the right to govern a particular country, man has shown an unfortunate leaning towards the usage of physical force.

Weapons have been devised according to the age; be they stone clubs, or high velocity rifles. The manner in which they were used has evolved too. The caveman who learned how to avoid his opponent's blows yet land his own effectively, lived to fight another day. Swordsmen who simply hacked at their opponents were soon despatched by those who developed the parry and riposte.

Regardless of the type of weapon, the means of using it has developed in line with greater expertise. This has been the case too with unarmed combat – where one's own body becomes a weapons system. The body has been the one thing that has remained relatively constant.

Having said that, you should not assume that there has been a constant development in unarmed combat from the Stone Age to the Plastic Age. For a start, there are only a limited number of things which the hands and feet can do, and secondly, the impetus to develop a system of unarmed combat has been irregular.

It is, after all, pointless to spend years learning a system of unarmed combat when the principal form of engagement uses swords. Therefore what has always tended to happen – at least in the military castes of history – is that the unarmed systems have been relegated to a fairly insignificant role. This is not the case in those other levels of society, where weapons are generally unavailable.

It comes as no surprise therefore, to learn that the most significant developments in unarmed combat have arisen in those societies where ordinary citizens were prohibited from bearing arms.

This is not to say that the military have totally ignored the development of unarmed combat, for even a disarmed soldier may be forced to fight on. Also, it is sometimes expedient to capture rather than to kill. It is for these reasons that the military castes of history have never completely abandoned unarmed combat.

In comparatively recent times, the warrior caste became divided into those who defend the state against armed incursion by foreigners (the military), and those who protect the state from its own citizens – i.e., the police. These differing roles require different weapons. Having said that, in present day armed societies, this distinction is becoming some-what blurred.

In principle, the police need to be able to take offenders into custody in such a way that the latter remain healthy enough to undergo judicial procedures. The problem with using potentially lethal weapons as deterrents when making an arrest is that at some stage, they may have to be used. Therefore so far as the average police force is concerned, non-lethal arrest systems are the most important.

These systems include the use of batons, staffs, and latterly high voltage stun-guns. Each weapon requires familiarisation training before it can be used to best effect. There is also a need for unarmed combat.

Members of the public need to protect themselves against criminals. The motive here is (or should be!) that of self defence. Unarmed combat is less important in those societies which permit the carrying of weapons.

Let me summarise the situation so far. Unarmed combat is, and has been practised, by:

- the military for emergency usage when the primary weapon cannot be deployed, and for the purposes of capture;

- the police, for arrest techniques and public order enforcement.

- the public, for usage against the violence inherent in any society.

The two principles of unarmed combat
Any form of unarmed combat relies upon just two principles. The first is the principle of landing a hard blow on the opponent's person. The second is the principle of applying force across a joint, or series of joints. Sufficient force applied to a joint causes actual or potential pain. It can even be used to unbalance an opponent.

Some time in the early history of mankind, it was discovered that when the testicles were struck sharply, the effect was out of all proportion to the actual force used. Since that time, other vulnerable points have been discovered. Less violent stimulation of certain vital points was claimed to have a healing effect, so many were mapped out in ancient eastern medical texts. Many points are now seen to correspond to local nerve networks. Some, when stimulated, produce their claimed effect in apparently quite unrelated parts of the body, yet modern embryology explains why this might be.

Provided you could hit a vulnerable point with the required level of force, victory was assured. This was fine in theory, but in practice, the opponent sometimes wore armour and seldom, if ever, remained still whilst you tried to poke at him!
A second line of impact development followed what I call 'the sledge-hammer theory'. This suggests that it doesn't matter which part of the opponent's body you strike, as long as you hit it with a lot of force. The sledgehammer theory relies upon conditioning the hands and feet so they become bludgeons, and then throwing those bludgeons with enough force to inflict the desired degree of damage.

Kicks and punches can be thrown by means of sheer muscle power, and/or by the application of physics. If muscle power was the only determining factor, then this form of unarmed combat would be useful only to large people. Fortunately it isn't the only factor. Skilled technique can lead to high acceleration, even over short distances. Ultimately however, acceleration reaches a maximum and any further gains then come from increased muscle power.

Some striking systems of unarmed combat use very little obvious muscle power, yet are effective nevertheless. These are sometimes referred to as 'soft', or 'internal', as opposed to the 'hard' or 'external' forms. Soft systems throw the fist or foot at the target, rather than drive it out using a lot of muscle power. The action is very fast, yet quite relaxed and it is only on impact that the muscles of the striking limb suddenly contract. As students of this system say, "it is important only to make the body weapon as heavy as possible, for it only takes a light blow with a sledgehammer to cause injury".

Leverage uses controlled force applied to a joint. Joints are clever pieces of biological machinery and when an external force tries to make them bend further than they were meant to, the result is pain! Pain is also caused when they are bent in a way which they were not designed to. Sophisticated forms of leverage apply a small force at the end of a long lever, rather than a large force at the end of a short lever.

The trick is using leverage to attack the most vulnerable joints, bearing in mind the relative strengths of both parties. People who are less strong should only attack weaker joints, such as those of the fingers, or wrist. When a hold fails, it is generally because the wrong joint has been attacked with insufficient leverage.

Normally people are blissfully unaware of the tremendous amount of unconscious neuromuscular activity required to keep them standing upright. Within limits, they cope with slight shifts in bodyweight but if leverage is skilfully applied, those limits are exceeded and they fall. Having said that, it is a very skilled person who can unbalance a poised and ready attacker. The rest of us must devise a means of 'catching the opponent off balance', and this too requires skill. Consider the following example.

Fred strikes the side of Jim's foot very hard. The result of this is only to make Fred hopping mad (excuse the pun!). If Fred tries to push Jim backwards and off balance, Jim will force himself forwards. Fred then suddenly pulls Jim towards him. The pull, plus Jim's own forwards push will make him step to retain balance. If Fred again strikes the side of Jim's foot, but this time as he is stepping, Jim will lose his balance and fall over.

This is obviously quite a sophisticated sequence, but it shows clearly that unarmed combat based on leverage alone needs a high level of skill. Compare this with the skill needed to be effective in an impact-based external system.

If time is of the essence, then the greatest short-term benefits in terms of effective unarmed combat will come from studying a system using blows. This is because it is easier to learn how to strike someone, than how to apply leverage. While this may suit the military and public, it is inappropriate for a police force.

The principle of yielding

When muscles are put to straining against each other, the ones which develop greater strength prevail. Therefore if you resist mightily when your attacker tries to drag you along, the confrontation will turn into a trial of strength.

Picture what would happen if you first resisted the opponent's pull, and then suddenly yielded and went with him. You might even switch from pulling against him, to actually pushing him! If the change is made quickly enough, you may succeed in unbalancing him.

The Japanese explained this concept by comparing the way in which trees respond to heavy winds. The oak stands firm, relying upon its great strength to protect it. The willow bows before the wind, and springs upright again as soon as the wind dies. The willow clearly expresses the concept of yielding.

Therefore if your opponent pulls you, push against him. If he pushes you back, pull him after you. Only a small amount of force used in this way, is needed to produce a large response.

Similarly if your opponent punches you, don't stand fast and match his blow with your block. First avoid the opponent's blow, then draw it out. so he is pulled off balance. When he is made vulnerable in this way, apply a suitable technique. The Japanese liken this to throwing a heavy stone into a thick curtain. The curtain moves with the stone and robs it of its force, so it falls harmlessly to the floor.

This sounds very efficient but unfortunately things are more complicated. The skilled opponent is more difficult to unbalance and less likely to over-extend his strikes. In such cases, you must dissipate his strength by distracting him with a striking technique to a vulnerable target. This allows you to apply your technique without having to wrestle with him.

The mysterious ki

You might think that the development of force for use in leverage or in a strike comes from the straightforward application of physical principles. A particular punch lands hard because it is delivered quickly by a large fist on the end of a beefy arm. A throw works because you unbalanced the opponent.

Yet many senior martial art teachers attribute a successful technique to what they call *ki*.

Ki is the Japanese word for a flow of energy through the body. Sometimes it is translated as 'spirit', or 'mind'. Those who believe in it claim that it can be used to increase the power of martial art techniques. The systems which use ki are invariably of the internal type, so practitioners move very quickly, yet seem to be relaxed.

The ability to control the flow of ki is said to come only after many years of practice, and for this reason, students were recommended to begin their study of martial arts with the external systems, turning to internal forms later in life. If this is true, then unarmed combat based upon internal systems would be ruled out for all except long-term students.

It is claimed that blows to certain areas where ki is said to be flowing, result in a break in the flow which may result in injury or death. Sometimes the onset of symptoms is delayed.

The power of ki has been demonstrated many times but some demonstrations at least, are frauds using simple physical principles to produce spectacular effects.

The Origins of Jiu Jitsu

The meaning of 'jiu jitsu'

Jiu jitsu is a Japanese martial art, the name meaning 'compliant techniques'. This refers to the way in which jiu jitsu momentarily yields to an attacker's force, redirects it and then snaps back with a counter-attack. Jiu jitsu incorporates both striking and leverage techniques, the former being generally used to create a distraction while a more powerful lock, hold or throw is applied.

I will use these three terms frequently, so it is as well if I explain them early on. A 'hold' is a way of restraining someone, so they are prevented from escaping, or continuing their attack. Strangleholds and chokes cut off the air and blood supply to the brain, so they quickly produce unconsciousness. A 'lock' is a hold applied to a joint; pressure is applied across the joint and pain is caused. In some cases, excessive force leads to dislocation of the joint and if this occurs at the neck or spine, death or permanent paralysis results.

A 'throw' is a method of taking the attacker to the floor by either moving his centre of gravity so he loses balance, or by applying a lock which forces him to the ground. If you keep hold of the attacker as he is thrown, you can firstly determine how he lands, and secondly perform a follow-up technique without delay.

Jiu jitsu makes use of the body's vulnerable points (known in Japanese as *kyusho* or *atemi*), both to cause injury, and to resuscitate an injured person. As you might imagine, knowledge of these could be dangerous in the wrong hands, so I make a point of not teaching them to anyone except the highest grades.

Jiu jitsu contains some non-Japanese techniques. It is claimed that the Chinese boxer named Chen Yuan-pin taught some Southern Chinese boxing to three leaderless samurai, and they subsequently incorporated his teachings into jiu jitsu.

Although nowadays jiu jitsu is mainly practised as a form of unarmed combat, it has not always been so. Many weapons are in fact associated with traditional practice, and I have described these later in the book. The problem lies in knowing just where to stop! The ancient Japanese warriors who developed jiu jitsu did not practise it as a discrete art. It was always taught in conjunction with other martial arts. The warrior might train with a sword, and then work at methods of disarming a sword-wielding soldier. He might train to use a dagger and then practise defence against it.

The police applications of jiu jitsu required non-lethal weapons such as the sais. The public were banned from carrying weapons, so their jiu jitsu incorporated so called 'covert weapons'. These were ostensibly agricultural or domestic implements, yet combined with jiu jitsu technique, they became effective weapons. The *bo* ('staff'), or *jo* ('stick') were capable of breaking a samurai's longsword.

Jiu jitsu has not stopped developing. New applications of technique constantly add to the syllabus. That is why the art itself will never become obsolete.

The climate in which jiu jitsu developed

To understand how jiu jitsu developed in Japan, it is necessary to know a little of the history of that country. Earliest traces of Japanese civilisation are found in the large *kofun* burial mounds, some of which are claimed to date back to prehistoric times. These traces take the form of pottery *haniwa* warriors and their horses. Some haniwa are so detailed, that the appearance of armour and protective helmet are easily seen. The haniwa warriors carry swords, and longbows.

The kofun mounds are the burial places of early leaders of tribes *(uji)*. The uji regarded their founders as gods, and the current leader was venerated both as king and priest. The most important uji claimed descent from Jimmu Tenno, the great-great grandson of the sun goddess Amaterasu. This warrior-king fought his way along the northern shores of the Inland Sea and established Japan's first capital city of Kyoto. Jimmu Tenno's line became the Japanese Imperial Family. Though not regarded as living gods, the emperor and his family were nevertheless regarded with awe and reverence. The emperor's status and political power reached its peak in the 5th century AD.

By the 8th century, a caste of trained warriors was beginning to emerge. Rather than conscripts taken from the fields, these were fervent fighting men who accepted discipline and fought because fighting was a part of their philosophy of life. These warriors were known as the *kondei*, or 'stalwart youth'.

Most of Japan is mountainous, with only one fifth being good agricultural land. In the main, this is distributed unevenly, though the flat plains surrounding Tokyo (Edo as it was known then) and Osaka were particularly fertile. The mountainous terrain made it difficult for any centralised form of government to establish itself and communities far from Kyoto governed themselves without interference.

As early as 200 AD, the Emperor Suijin was obliged to grant a temporary commission for a military commander-in-chief in order to further his military ambitions. The rank conferred by this commission was known as *shogun*, and it was surrendered at the completion of the assigned task. However, the commission ceased to be temporary and as power transferred from the emperor to the warlords, the shogun emerged as the most powerful man in all Japan.

Provincial communities grew up around warrior families, the latter being known as the *bushi dan*. Bushi dan consisted of the head of the family, his male relatives and their families. Unrelated young warriors were also included and referred to as the *kenin*, this term meaning 'those who live in the house'. Neighbouring uji competed with one another for land, wealth and status. The measure of an uji's wealth was the number of *koku* his land could generate, a koku being the quantity of rice needed to feed a man for a year.

Hard frontier-type existence forged tough and resourceful warriors, whose first allegiance was to the head of the tribe. The emperor ruled by consent of the tribal chiefs, and incidences of disobedience were by no means infrequent. Perhaps the most significant involved Taira Masakado who, in 935 AD, rose in open revolt against the Kyoto government. Taira Masakado was related to the Emperor Kammu who ruled Japan in the period 781-806 AD, so this gave him stature, at least in his eastern domain.

The rebellion was put down after 5 gruelling years of warfare. Taira Masakado was vanquished by his first cousin, who fought on the side of the emperor not so much from motives of patriotism, as for revenge against the killing of his father. The Kyoto-based government was victorious only because it was able to enlist the aid of provincial lords *(daimyo)* and their private armies of warriors.

The power of the daimyo continued to grow at the expense of the Kyoto government, and soon even the Buddhist monasteries were arming themselves. The concept of hereditary warriors, or bushi was established, with individual status related to ancestry and prestige of the domain governed by a bushi family.

Assisting the bushi were retainers who were referred to as *samurai* (literally, 'one who serves'). At first these functioned merely as squires but in the 14th century, they came to be regarded as warriors in their own right.

A code of conduct known as *kyuba no-michi* was adopted, and later this became known as *bushido*, the 'way of the warrior'.

The eleventh century ushered in a conflict between the two leading Japanese clans, the Taira and the Minamoto. The Taira clan had control of the emperor but life at court had made its warriors weak. This was to tell in the decisive encounter at Dan no-ura in April 1185, when the Minamoto forces triumphed. During the battle at the Straits of Shimonoseki, the boy emperor, Antoku Tenno was drowned when his grandmother, carrying him in her arms, jumped from their ship to prevent him falling into the hands of the Minamoto.

Minamoto Yoritomo (1147-99) was declared the first permanent shogun in 1192. He was determined that his warriors would not become weak through court living, so he set up the headquarters of his military government *(bakufu)* in Kamakura. The bakufu represented a government of warriors for warriors and through a gradual process, its authority was increased until it exceeded that of the imperial court.

Minamoto Yoritomo well realised that the diamyo could not be wooed by appeals to their loyalty, for their only loyalty was to themselves. He ruled instead by appealing to their greed, rewarding service with gifts of land. Even those who had opposed him were invited to serve in the bakufu because the shogun valued their martial art skills and had no wish to see them wasted. Loyalty was gradually built up and those who did not give of it unstintingly were invited to commit suicide *(seppuku)*. The coarse name for this is *hara kiri*, which means 'belly-slitting'.

When Yoritomo died in 1199, the Hojo Family supervised his two sons, Yorii and Sanetomo. These proved to be incompetent shoguns, unable to gain the support of the daimyo. Yorii was exiled and then assassinated by the Hojo. Sanetomo was murdered by his nephew. They were succeeded by Hojo nominees, none of whom were of bushi stock. As such they did not hold the respect and obedience of the daimyos. To maintain power, the Hojo regents offered posts in the bakufu so loyalty was gradually taken from the shogun, and vested in the bakufu itself.

Dissention broke out between the daimyos and it was only the Mongol invasions in the late 13th century that prevented the bakufu from falling apart. The Hojo shogunate was finally overthrown in 1333 by imperial forces assisted by Ashikaga Takauji. Ashikaga was later established as shogun amidst much enthusiasm for his bushi status. Despite this, he proved to be a corrupt and inept ruler. Under Ashikaga government (1336-1568), the bakufu gradually lost its control over the country and anarchy prevailed, with every man for himself.

In the absence of law, right of might became overwhelmingly important and the daimyos increased the size of their private armies by conscripting peasants. These were known as the *no-bushi*, or 'field warriors'. In times of danger, even farmers were called up and these came to be known as the *ji samurai*, or 'farmer-warriors'. The professional warrior class was no longer the only part of society allowed to bear arms. Even so, only the true bushi were permitted to carry two swords; no-bushi and ji samurai had to be content with one short-sword.

The Portuguese arrived during the mid 16th century, bringing firearms with them. These caused uproar within the Japanese military establishment, because amongst other things, they offended the very spirit of honourable combat. Nevertheless, at the battle of Nagashino in 1575, Oda Nobunaga's conscript army defeated an army of traditional warriors under the command of Takeda Katsuyori.

The new martial art of the musket was known as *ho jutsu*, or 'firing techniques'. It took far less time to train a conscript to fire a musket than it did to produce a classical warrior trained in the use of the sword, bow and spear.

The power of the Ashikaga shogunate had diminished to zero when Oda moved in on Kyoto, but his triumph was shortlived – he was assassinated by one of his aides. His place was taken by another aide – Toyotomi Hideyoshi (1536-98). Toyotomi avenged Oda's death during the battle of Yamazaki and then went on to install himself as shogun. One of his edicts forbade the carrying of weapons by peasants and farmers. Another bound the warriors to their daimyos.

Following a decisive battle at Sekigahara in 1600, Toyotomi was succeeded by Tokugawa Ieyasu (1542-1616). The Tokugawa shogunate ushered in a period of peace, during which the classical martial arts fell into disuse. Practical martial art techniques became changed, and many rituals were added. By this means, *bu jutsu*, the techniques of martial art, became *budo*, the way of martial art and the bushi diverted thereby into less warlike pastimes.

The Tokugawa bakufu was run almost entirely by civilian officials and by less scrupulous bushi. Control over the population passed into the hands of a police force which was equipped to disarm and restrain offenders, rather than simply to kill them. The declining ability of Tokugawa warriors made it relatively easy to capture them, something that would have been almost impossible even a short time ago.

The end of the Tokugawa shogunate came soon after the arrival at Uraga, on 8th July 1853, of four ships under Commodore Perry. From that time onwards, the bakufu's influence declined rapidly and the period 1853-1868 became known as the *bakumatsu*, or 'end of the bakufu'.

The 15th and last Tokugawa shogun, Keiki, was defeated in the civil war of 1866 and persuaded to hand back his commission to the Emperor Mitsuhito (Meiji). In 1868, the emperor published a proclamation in which he assumed all the ex-shogun's power. This became known as the 'Meiji Restoration'.

During the restoration, all civilians were disarmed and practice of the martial arts all but died out.

The do and the jutsu forms
The incessant warfare between the 8th and 16th centuries provided the ideal testing ground for military technique. Those which survived, became incorporated into a tradition known as the *ryu*.

The ryu of *bujutsu* (martial art techniques), were open only to the warrior elite. They concerned themselves with hand-to-hand combat and many of the techniques used were so dangerous that they could only be practised through prearranged performances known as *kata*. The concept underlying classical bujutsu was that one man would win, and another would pay for that victory with his life.

The budo (martial art ways) developed during the relative peace of the Tokugawa shogunate. Though budo techniques were based upon those used in bujutsu, they weren't practised in the same way. With opportunities for combat severely restricted, budo came to be practised as a form of physical exercise, or sport. The object in practice was for the warrior to conquer his own ego.

One could perhaps summarise and simplify the difference between the two by saying that jutsu forms were concerned with defeating the opponent; budo forms were concerned with defeating one's self.

The history of jiu jitsu
The Nihon Shoki chronicle of 720 AD records how, in 23 BC, the Emperor Suinjin held a martial art tournament to celebrate the seventh year of his reign. One of the bouts resulted in the death of a participant when he was thrown and then kicked. Sumo wrestling developed from these early tournaments, and though there is a common ancestry, jiu

jitsu and sumo are not related. One essential difference is that sumo is a sport whereas jiu jitsu remained a battlefield art.

Annual tournaments were held during the reign of the Emperor Minmyo (833-845 AD), and in the mid 9th century, the sixth son of Emperor Fukiwara started a line of development which eventually gave rise to the *Daito ryu aiki-jiu jitsu*.

Perhaps the first reference to a jiu jitsu-like form of combat is found in the 15th century martial art tradition known as the *Katori shinto ryu*. It was known there as *yawarra-ge* ('pacifier') and was used as a support system for the longsword. The similarly named *yawarra-gi* ('meekness') consisted of 100 techniques and formed part of the syllabus of the *Muso jikiden ryu*.

Also of the 15th century Tsutsumi-hozan ryu was the first to study and systematise grappling in full armour under the title of *yoroi kumi-uchi*. The roots of this system are found in the more primitive early grappling systems mentioned above.

Yoroi kumi-uchi was employed when it was not possible to use the sword. The warriors closed range and grappled with each other whilst trying to drive a special blade known as the *yoroi-doshi* through joints in the armour. *Hojo jutsu*, the 'techniques of tying' went hand in glove with yoroi kumi-uchi. These used the cord that each warrior carried, to single-handedly bind the struggling opponent.

The *Takenouchi ryu* developed a system which they named *Kogusoku*, for use by lightly armoured warriors carrying just a short sword. Later this became known as *tori-te*. Not to be outdone, the *Yagyu shrinkage ryu* developed a system of grappling which could be used both by armoured and unarmoured warriors.

The famous swordsman Miyamoto Musashi studied a form of yawarra-ge named *Kakushi-jutsu* which specialised in the usage of concealed weapons.

In the early 17th century, the swordsman Nagao Kemmotsu developed a school of what was termed *Tai jutsu* ('body techniques'). This too involved the usage of hidden weapons. At the same time, Oguri Niemon developed a form of grappling which could be used by people in street clothes. He intended this to be used during times of peace, naming it *wa jutsu*, or 'techniques of softness'.

All these various systems can be brought together under the general heading of *kumi-uchi*. From this, what we now refer to as jiu jitsu was developed.

The 15th century saw the development of military infiltration techniques known as *Ninjutsu* (the 'techniques of stealth'). Ninjutsu was an entire but covert martial art which was strictly comparable to the more orthodox fighting systems of feudal Japan. It produced a class of specialist warriors known as the *ninja*, whose legendary feats have passed into folklore.

Ninja were used when circumstances precluded an overt military operation. Their successful deployment depended upon a number of factors, the first being knowledge of the target's whereabouts and future plans. This was obtained by observation, and by paid informers. The ninja were skilled in the use of camouflage and it was claimed they could remain motionless for many hours. They wore no armour and dressed according to the type of operation, so at night, they wrapped themselves from head to foot with dark clothing, exposing only the eyes.

Their senses were trained to such a degree that they could detect the target's movement in poor light, and by listening to the background noise of night creatures, discover if anyone was passing nearby.

Next, the ninja needed to reach the target, using such methods as riding, swimming, scaling walls, or by worming through narrow gaps. Ninja trained with cloth-bound grappling hooks and practised dropping silently and safely from great heights. It was claimed that they could walk over sprung wooden floors in the dead of night without raising an alarm.

Ninja engaged in a long term operation infiltrated the target's house-hold, taking on the role of a servant. Once in position, they would wait for the right moment and then strike. If cornered, their ability was such that they could take on samurai in direct attack. They invariably committed suicide in the face of capture, since it was unthinkable that they should betray their lord.

If the objective was to capture the target, then ninja used unarmed combat techniques which are now incorporated within the jiu jitsu syllabus. They also used *hojo jutsu*, which are the 'techniques of trying' an opponent. Drugs were sometimes used to incapacitate the victim.

The ninja's weapons suited their manner of operation, being designed to kill quickly and silently. The warrior's longsword was unmanageable in enclosed spaces, so the ninja used a shorter and lighter version. Main weapons however, were the knife and the garrotte. A short spear was also favoured but this, like the bow and arrow, was only used once the attack had been discovered. Ninja 'throwing stars' and spiked caltrops scattered over the floor of a corridor were used to harass the defenders and delay pursuit.

Ninja operated both alone, and in small groups trained to work as a unit. Like any military operation, each ninja was given a specific task and in the event of a disengagement whilst under attack, other ninja gave covering fire from hidden positions. Smoke bombs and other such devices were used to cause panic. Sometimes a group of ninja would act as decoys, distracting the defenders' attention and so exposing the target to attack.

The establishment of the Tokugawa shogunate and the suppression of warfare led to an increase in the level of ninja activity. Some ninja were retained by the shogunate to act as secret police and as military prowess declined, non-military ninja began to appear. These were mercenaries, contract killers, spies and informers who could sometimes be persuaded to slip poison into the victim's food. Some were sufficiently courageous to knife the victim in the back. They simply worked for money – something that no self-respecting samurai would ever do.

These mercenary ninja were normally contacted through a retainer of the person seeking to employ them. Someone always knew 'someone else' who might be prepared to arrange a contact.

The fighting advantage (if any) of these later ninja was conferred through surprise and the usage of atypical weapons with which the samurai were unfamiliar. However in a face-to-face confrontation, the outcome was almost certain victory for the warriors. Since these ninja were not from a military tradition, there was no warrior ethic to their training

Ninja organisations promoted belief in their supernatural powers and referred to *Kuji kiri* ('nine hands cutting') in which the body's powers were focussed in preparation for action. This, it was claimed, resulted in invisibility and the ability to scale sheer walls.

The title jiu jitsu was first used during the late 17th century, under the Tokugawa shogunate. The system was developed in response to the needs of that society and as armour was gradually phased out, so the content of the training syllabus changed accordingly. The system became known colloquially as *yawarra* ('resilience' or 'flexibility').

The first entirely weaponless jiu jitsu school was opened by a samurai named Terada Kanemon. He narrowed down the classical bujutsu martial tradition of the Kito ryu to a purely weaponless school which he called the *Jikishin ryu*. The system he taught was named *judo* ('compliant techniques'). This is not to be confused with Jigoro Kano's judo which came into being nearly a century later.

During the first half of the 19th century, Iso Mataemon studied two classical ryu and took from them a study of striking techniques to the body's vulnerable points. He named his school the *Tenjin shinyo ryu*. Mataemon taught his students never to waste their energy in a loud shout, but to *kiai* with a closed mouth. This principle has been carried through to the present day.

The Meiji Restoration was a period in which Japan's interests turned westward, and the traditional martial arts fell into a decline. Nevertheless, attempts were made to keep them in being and in 1895, bujutsu and budo ryu formed the Dai-Nihon Butokukai. This was centred around the famous Butokuden training hall.

Jigoro Kano was born in 1860 and began his study of the martial arts at the age of 17, by enrolling in the Tenjin shinyo ryu school of jiu jitsu. His first teacher was Fukuda Hachinosuke and when the latter died, he joined the Kito ryu in 1881 and trained under Ikubo Tsunetoshi. He therefore received a good grounding in both striking and grappling/throwing techniques.

A programme of study brought him into contact with two bujutsu ryu, namely the *Sekiguchi ryu* and the *Seigo ryu*. The result of this combination of practice and theory was the founding in 1882 of the martial way of *Kodokan judo*. Kano chose the suffix do to emphasize the philosophical

18

nature of his system. Despite the success of judo in becoming an olympic sport, other schools of jiu jitsu still practise.

Jiu jitsu was first introduced to Britain during the last years of the 19th century by Japanese students, seamen, soldiers and business men. In the early 20th century, a Tenjin shinyo ryu instructor by the name of Yukio Tani came to Britain and went into business with W. Barton-Wright. They tried to open a jiu jitsu academy but this failed through lack of publicity.

For a while, Tani gave demonstrations of jiu jitsu in music halls under his stage name 'the Pocket Hercules', then he went into business with William Bankier and opened the Japanese school of jiu jitsu in Oxford St. The British Jiu Jitsu Society was set up and a magazine published to bring the art to the notice of the public.

Two other Japanese instructors visited Britain at around the same period. Sada Uyenishi wrote an English language book about jiu jitsu, and trained with Tani. Taru Miyake arrived later and defeated Tani in a contest. For a time, both Tani and Miyake taught at the Oxford St. club. Gunji Koizumi came to Britain in 1906 and taught members of the armed services. In 1918, he opened the Budokwai and asked Yukio Tani to be its chief instructor. The Budokwai subsequently became a centre for Japanese culture.

Tani was assisted by William Steers, a pupil of Uyenishi and the first Englishman to attain first dan rank in Kodokan judo. E.J. Harrison was the second ever English black belt. He campaigned vigorously for the Budokwai to concentrate upon the teaching of Kodokan judo. Jigoro Kano visited the Budokwai in 1920 and conferred upon it the mandate to govern Kodokan judo. Judo was promoted as the most developed form of jiu jitsu and as a result, many jiu jitsu clubs joined the Budokwai – even though some retained their original form of practice. The British Jiu Jitsu Society did not affiliate to the Budokwai.

Just before the Second World War, the martial arts returned to favour in Japan, because it was considered that their practice increased conscripts' military enthusiasm. Judo was banned after the war for precisely this reason.

When this prohibition was finally lifted, large numbers of servicemen began training and carried the seeds of jiu jitsu's international development back to their own countries.

The jiu jitsu practised today can be separated into three types. These are:

(a) Traditional jiu jitsu such as that based upon the kumiuchi of the bujutsu ryu.

(b) Japanese non-traditional jiu jitsu (Nihon goshin jiu jitsu) which was based upon later, unarmed forms. The Hakko ryu school which was founded in 1948, is an example of this category.

(c) Non-Japanese, non-traditional jiu jitsu which is based upon the teaching of Japanese non-traditional schools.

Weapons Used in Jiu Jitsu

As you will have gathered from the previous chapter, jiu jitsu does involve weapon usage, though this aspect diminished in the early 18th century. However no account of jiu jitsu can afford to ignore the importance of weapons to classical training. The following is a description of the weapons which have been associated with jiu jitsu.

The sword

To the classical warrior, the sword was more than simply a weapon. It was a symbol of justice, cutting down evil and enforcing the law. The classical warrior used it without rancour, anger, or cruelty. His attitude was that of a surgeon cutting out a malignant growth in order that the patient might live.

The Japanese sword can be used one-handed though it is more usual to use both hands. It is a single-edged weapon with a sharp, stabbing point. The tip was originally sharpened as one with the blade but the Mongol chainmail armour worn during the invasions of 1274 and 1281, caused it to break off and damage the blade. This was later solved by sharpening the edge and tip separately.

Various sizes of sword were used at different times. The *tachi* was a long-sword worn from the hip and carried with the cutting edge downwards-facing. This meant that it was drawn high into the air, so as to be brought down upon the target; an advantage when using it from horse-back. The *katana* was smaller and lighter, so it could be used more quickly. This was worn with the cutting edge facing upwards, making it possible to slash out immediately the sword left the sheath.

The *wakizashi* also called the *kodachi*) was a smaller sword entirely, and intended for use with one hand. It was used to best advantage in confined spaces, or as a support for the longsword in the kenjutsu system known as *nito*. The warrior wore the wakizashi tucked into his waistband next to the katana in the combination known as *daisho* (meaning 'one large, one small').

Earliest Japanese swords are known to have been forged as early as 200 BC but it was not until 700 AD that the familiar curved shape emerged. During the 16th century, Korean metalworkers were brought to Japan and demonstrated a process known as 'compression forging', by which means the blades were made incredibly dense and tough.

Red hot steel ingots were cut almost in half, then folded lengthways and hammered out. This process was repeated several times with the result that the steel became densely layered and incredibly strong. The blade was then shaped to its final form and tempered.

The tempering process was another key factor leading to a hard yet resilient blade. The blade was heated to the correct temperature and then quenched in cool water. The tempered blade was then sent away for sharpening and polishing.

The finished blade was fitted with a temporary wooden handle and tested on the bodies of condemned criminals. Blades which passed this gruesome test were certificated by the shogun's appointee and then handed over to their new owners.

The techniques of sword usage are known as *kenjutsu*. It is claimed that around 5,000 ryu practised kenjutsu techniques, the first recorded being the *Tenshin shoden katori shinto ryu* which was originated in the 15th century by Choisai Izasa Ienao.

Iaijutsu is the name given to sword drawing and sheathing techniques. Far from being ritualistic, these techniques conferred a real advantage on the skilled warrior by giving him the chance to make the first cut. Exponents practised drawing the sword from a variety of positions – seated, standing, etc. The object was to bring the blade into effective play in the shortest possible time after it had cleared the scabbard.

The sword was a close distance weapon, so antagonists could use kicks, trips, or even grapples. That pioneer of British Kendo, R.A. Lidstone described how in a spirited bout, he lost his bamboo practice sword *(shinai)* but unperturbed, he charged his surprised opponent. The pair of them went over the back of a wicker chair, much to the consternation of an audience of dignified visitors. Lidstone reported that he managed to apply a kumi-uchi lock which caused the opponent to submit!

The knife

Depending upon its length, the Japanese knife is known as the *tanto*. Like the sword, the knife is single edged and slightly curved, being more suited to cutting or slashing than stabbing. As has been previously mentioned, the *yoroi doshi* dagger was used during grappling, to attack weak points in the opponent's armour.

The knife is a shorter range weapon than the sword, so in the techniques of the bujutsu ryu, it was taught in conjunction with chokes and holds. The Takenouchi ryu used knife techniques during kogusoku grappling.

Many jiu jitsu schools taught defence against knife attack.

The spear

The spear *(yari)* consists of a long, hardwood pole with a piercing metal tip. The tip is attached by binding the tang into the pole.

The spear is a long range weapon, so training with it involved few jiu jitsu related moves. Having said that, Sekiguchi Jushin, the founder of the *Sekiguchi ryu*, devised yawarra grappling techniques which would work against a warrior brandishing a spear.

Even in classical spear training, the butt was used to attack weak spots in the armour.

The halberd

Japanese halberds (called *nagamaki* or *naginata*) were first used as anti-cavalry weapons but when horses became scarce, they were relegated to specialist or home defence weapons. As with the spear, they were used from a distance which made closing and grappling very difficult.

The staff

The hardwood 2 metre staff was not a widely used weapon of the classical warrior because it was regarded as too humble. Nevertheless, 300 ryu incorporated staff techniques, or *bojutsu* into their syllabus. The first recorded such development occurred in the Tenshin shoden katori shinto ryu. Non-military schools of bojutsu also developed and Buddhist monks in particular developed techniques to a high degree.

The staff can be swung at the opponent, or used to jab at him. Because of the dense wood used in its construction, the staff develops a lot of power and I have seen a single swipe inadvertently destroy a well made wooden chair. It is said that a blow from the staff could shatter a sword blade.

Staff fighting involved some short distance work, during which kicks and trips were used.

The stick

The hardwood stick *(jo)* is shorter than the staff, and can be swung about more quickly. Indeed, one aiki-jiu jitsu teacher was said to be able to weave an impenetrable defence around himself by means of a rapidly moving jo. The 17th century *Shindo muso ryu* was the starting point for a subsequent development of more than seventy styles of *jojutsu* ('stick techniques').

The jo can be used with a swinging or jabbing action. It is also used to apply locks to the shoulder and elbow joints.

The truncheon

The short stick, or truncheon, is a close range weapon, often used in conjunction with grappling techniques. Typically it is used in a clubbing, thrusting, or blocking action, often against the opponent's weak spots. The truncheon is a police weapon and was introduced to Japan after the Second World War. A syllabus of effective techniques using it were built up by referring to the 17th century *Ikaku ryu*. This tradition taught usage of the *jutte* (a single-tined iron truncheon).

Jutte are not readily available nowadays, so some jiu jitsu schools have 'adopted' the Okinawan *sai*. This is a three pronged truncheon, with the central tine considerably longer than the two laterals. The sai were used by Okinawan militia to quell an unruly suspect and they could be used to reinforce the forearm, making it possible to block swings made with a staff. It was said that true experts, armed with a pair of sai, were capable of defending themselves against a Tokugawa warrior armed with a sword.

The Okinawan rice grinder handles known as *tonfa* have also attracted much attention in non-traditional jiu jitsu schools. These consist of a hardwood baton, with a peg jutting out nearer one end than the other. The peg allows the baton to be viciously swung in an arc, from a position of guard alongside the forearm. The tonfa's 'heel' projects forward from guard position, giving added range and impact to a strike.

American police who are concurrently martial artists, have introduced the tonfa to modern police work. Police tonfas are made of an aluminium alloy and some carry a bright torch in the heel.

The rice flail *(nunchaku)*, made famous in Bruce Lee films, has also been imported into modern jiu jitsu practice. This weapon consists of a pair of batons linked by chain or thong. They can be used like an orthodox truncheon, or they can be swung through the air with one baton held and the other free. The linking chain or thong can be used to trap a limb, or to apply a stranglehold.

The fan

The iron fan, or *tessen*, was a disguised weapon which could be taken by the visitor into a house without causing offence. It resembled the normal fan and some actually opened out. Typically however, the tessen was a strip of iron, shaped and painted to look like a fan.

The tessen was typically a weapon of defence, parrying knife cuts and striking back at the hand holding the knife. It could be used as a club, or simply jabbed at the opponent's vulnerable areas.

The sickle and chain

The farmer's sickle *(kama)* was a covert self defence weapon used by monks, peasants and farmers. It was never intended to compete effectively against a sword-wielding warrior. The kama consisted of a slightly curved, single edged blade firmly attached to a heavy hardwood handle, making it possible to cut, pierce, or to club the opponent.

By attaching a light chain with a weight at one end to the sickle, a composite weapon known as the *kusarigama* was made. The chain allowed the user to ensnare an opponent, after which he could be finished off with the sickle. This however, called for great dexterity which could only be obtained after years of training.

The first school known to teach the techniques of kusarigama *(kusarigama jutsu)* was the *Ishin ryu*. This was founded by a buddhist monk named Jion.

Knuckledusters

Knuckledusters *(tekki)* were used to strike the body's vulnerable points. They could be easily concealed and so proved popular when weapons were forbidden to all except the military.

The *Nagao ryu* used a knuckleduster in the form of a metal ring. This was known as a *tekkan-zu*.

The Philosophy of Jiu Jitsu

The martial spirit

The development of traditional jiu jitsu took place, as you have read, during a time of constant warfare. Far from merely accepting death, samurai were urged to embrace it. Consider the words of the Hagakure Bushido, written by the monk Yamamoto Tsunetomo in the early 18th century:

> *"Bushido, I have found out, lies in dying . . . When confronted with two alternatives, life or death, one is to choose death without hesitation . . . Think of oneself as already dead . . . Once 'dead', one's energy and attention are set free to pass directly to the fulfillment of his purpose."*

The Tokugawa shogunate reduced the incidence of warfare and lowered the martial spirit. Warriors were taught to defeat their own egos, rather than the opponent through study of what are called the *do* ('way', as in 'way to follow') forms of martial art practice. Instead of generating aggression, these actually sought to reduce it.

The student of the 'way' accepted an inferior status, performing such menial tasks as sweeping the training hall and fetching water. Training was deliberately hard, repetitive, uncompromising and in some cases downright sadistic. Students were taught little, being made to repeat elementary techniques over and over again. The object in doing all this was to produce a small number of martial artists without regard or ambition for self.

Without the correct mental attitude, there was little point in practising any martial art. The coward worries about what may happen to him and this slows his reaction and clouds his mind. In his imagination, he sees himself losing the encounter even before it actually happens. He is riddled with self-doubt and lacks the motivation to respond correctly. He may be superbly fit and highly competent. Yet he is convinced that he cannot win. Why is that?

Many martial artists have an inaccurate impression of themselves. Some think they are very good, when in fact they are not. Others think they are poor martial artists when they are actually quite competent.

Martial artists often wrongly assess the calibre of the opponent, seeing him tougher or more resolute than he really is. This is perhaps marginally safer than underestimating him. The opponent's ability is not as important a factor as one might think. Everyone has read about weak people defeating stronger attackers. This is not an isolated phenomenon.

The motivation to fight back and to succeed has nothing at all to do with anger. Anger is a negative emotion, destroying coordination between mind and body, so skill is lost and judgement impaired. The most deadly exponents of martial art remain frighteningly cool; almost detached in their attitude. If the mind is calm, the techniques work to their maximum effect.

Any reasonably fit person can learn the techniques of jiu jitsu and become skilled in their application, but this merely makes them into technicians. A martial artist is a technically proficient person who has adopted the correct mental attitude.

Many students learn the physical techniques of jiu jitsu to a high standard, but very few actually learn the martial art itself. This fact reveals itself in the squabblings and politics which so plague modern martial art practice.

The philosophy of practice
In the purely physical sense of the word, jiu jitsu techniques are effective. They did not suffer as badly as some martial arts from the changes imposed during the Tokugawa Shogunate.

Constant practice sets up what are called 'neuromuscular pathways' and these are needed to produce the sometimes quite complicated jiu jitsu techniques. At first the student divides a technique into a series of manageable sub-stages and concentrates on getting them in the correct order. After a lot of practice, he is able to run a couple of sub-stages together and finally, he can perform the whole technique without hesitation.

Once the mechanics of the technique are learned, application can be studied. Further practice refines both mechanics and application still further, until the technique becomes an expression of art. After practising over a long period, faultless execution becomes automatic and the student literally 'forgets' technique until the right stimulus occurs. Absence of conscious selection and control makes response very fast indeed.

Once learned, no technique is ever actually forgotten, though if for any reason practice ceases, speed and skill levels begin dropping almost immediately. This is why even the most advanced students of jiu jitsu constantly practise basic techniques. A bad student loses interest after repeating a technique, and wants to learn something new. This is an incorrect attitude. Basic techniques must be mastered before going on to more advanced ones.

It is not simply a matter of learning a new technique. Some techniques may need a level of flexibility or co-ordination before they can be applied. Often this is trained-in by repeating basic techniques. All training must be related to the syllabus, and the student's degree of advancement.

The jiu jitsu way
Training begins and ends with courtesy. Everyone is learning together; it is just that some are a little further along the path than others.

Respect is a cornerstone of jiu jitsu. If the student does not respect the teacher or his classmates, how can he respect himself? If the teacher does not respect his students, then why does he teach them?

The training hall may be a custom-built dojo, or a room in a sports centre. It doesn't matter, because wherever jiu jitsu students train, they are in a dojo, or place for following the way of martial art.

It is customary to show respect for the dojo. Before entering, students slip off their footwear at the edge of the training mat and bow from a standing position, hands flat to the side of the training uniform. The bow is slow and measured, with a hesitation at the lowest point. The student always bows on entering and leaving the training area, directing the bow towards the teacher, or towards a senior grade. If no one is present, then the bow is made towards the centre of the dojo. No student should leave the dojo unless they have permission from the teacher.

Behaviour in the dojo can be summed up in one word – moderate. Students should not speak unless they are spoken to by the teacher. They should converse between themselves only when necessary, and then only in a low voice. When a technique is being demonstrated, they should stand attentively and not slouch, or prop themselves against walls. They must tuck their feet in when they sit down, and keep their backs erect. All commands by the teacher, or by class seniors must be obeyed quickly.

Everyone wears the same training uniform *(gi)* and it is not possible for one student to look better kitted-out than another. This promotes unity and removes barriers. Students must demonstrate self respect by wearing clean and well-pressed training tunics. All rips and tears must be repaired.

Long hair must be held back with an elastic band and the finger- and toenails kept clean and short. Students are in close contact with one another, so personal hygiene is important. Excessive makeup should be avoided. Earrings, rings and necklaces may not be worn since they are a danger not only to the wearer but also to the partners.

Spectacles may not be worn during training, though they may be slipped on in order to see a technique being demonstrated. Soft contact lenses are worn on the wearer's own responsibility.

The student is expected to train hard, and to show courage in the execution of techniques. The teacher *(sensei)* will not expect one student to defeat another, but to surpass instead his own standard of yesterday. Jiu jitsu uses a system of coloured belts to demonstrate progress in skill and knowledge. This is not a traditional practice but it is justified perhaps in the effort it wrings from students. It is however, a bad thing to train only in order to win a higher grade.

From a traditional point of view, it may be that gradings are a bad thing. However, in the absence of life-or-death combat, some form of measurement is useful. The grading is effective because it identifies a goal worth achieving, and a realistic timescale in which to achieve it. Success does not depend upon circumstances outside of the students' control.

Ultimately, the status of the student is reflected in the quality and frequency of his training.

This chapter opened with a reference to the Hagakure Bushido and it is appropriate to close it with another quotation. This comes from Yagyu Tajima no-kami Muenori (1571-1646), the founder of the *Yagyu shinkage ryu* and official instructor of kenjutsu to the Tokugawa shogunate:

> *'Lifetime training knows no end. One has to find himself improved after each day's training; striving towards perfection for the entire course of his life.'*

Preparing for Training

Fitness

If students are reasonably fit, then they will gain more benefit from their training. They will be able to practise vigorously for the whole of the lesson without running out of energy. It will be possible to concentrate on technique and not be distracted by shortness of breath, or by aches and pains resulting from a hard session.

I have always believed that the best fitness training for jiu jitsu is jiu jitsu itself. That is why, in these pages, scant reference is made to additional exercises. This is not to say that such exercises are valueless, but merely that there is no sense in taking up space in a manual of jiu jitsu with exercises which can be obtained from any book on general fitness.

Jiu jitsu students come from many walks of life. Some work with their hands, others with their heads. When they come to training, their heads are filled with the day's distractions, so the first thing to do is to narrow their attention down to the requirements of practice. This can be achieved by mental and physical exercises before training proper begins.

Mental exercise comes from such things as meditation, or by mentally rehearsing techniques. Physical exercises rehearse the body for the demands that jiu jitsu training will place upon it. Running on the spot raises the body's level of activity, increasing the rate of heart-beat and breathing. As the muscles work, they generate heat and this shows itself in the feeling of warmth that soon sets in. The object however, is to warm up but not to tire out the students.

Running on the spot can be followed by arm-circling, so the shoulder joints are put through their full range of movement. Wrists must be extended and flexed, then moved from side to side. The spine must be made to bend and twist to the limits of movement. The hip joint is worked by bending and raising the knee to the front and to the side, then by moving the knee joint in large circles; first in one direction, then in the other. The ankle joints are worked by standing on tiptoe, then the heels are dropped by standing on a step. Finally, the feet are rolled outwards and inwards.

All joint movement work is performed in a gentle way, using no more than body weight. The joint to be exercised is taken through its full range of movement and as the limit is approached, no further force is applied. The joint is held near the limit of comfortable stretch for at least 10 seconds before being relaxed.

The object in doing this is to stretch the muscles which act across the joints, since it is mainly these which determine how far a limb can move. Under no circumstances should students be allowed to jerk on the muscles being stretched because this triggers a reflex contraction which prevents further stretching from taking place.

All work done during warm up is of a general nature. More specific exercises should be used afterwards. Physical shortcomings will become obvious as training progresses and these should be remedied by specific exercises when the body is thoroughly warmed up.

The reason for a cool down after training is that activities performed in the training hall are unsuitable for the street and so the body and mind must be returned to a state suitable for coping with everyday life once more. This can be brought about by meditation.

The muscles have been working throughout the training session and will be full of the waste products of energy production. Within a short time after training finishes, the blood supply to muscles is reduced and any waste materials left behind are effectively 'locked up'. If these are not removed, then the muscles become stiff and achey. Therefore cool down must take place immediately after training.

Falling safely

Jiu jitsu involves throwing techniques. Therefore it is necessary to learn how to fall safely before training proper can begin. There is one secret to falling safely and that is, to relax the body. The person who hits the floor with the muscles of his body relaxed is less likely to suffer injury than the person who is stiff and unyielding.

Students are understandably nervous about landing hard on the floor, so a practice-progression is used to build up confidence. Even then, if a landing is less than satisfactory, the training mat is very effective at soaking up and dissipating energy, so an injury is unlikely.

Practice begins from a crouched position, with hands extended forwards (*fig 1*). The student falls backwards onto the mat, curving his spine as he does so. His head is tucked forwards and his chin is brought into his chest. Downwards motion is converted into a roll back onto the shoulders, and both arms slap palm-down on the mat to kill additional energy (*fig 2*). Very soon, the student tackles this exercise with confidence and is ready to try it from a slightly higher stance. Eventually, it can be performed from an upright position.

FIG 1

FIG 2

In all cases, the fall must be translated into a rolling motion, and it is for this reason that the spine is always curved. The head must be brought forward, so it does not bang against the mat.

From the same crouching position, the student reaches forward and grasps the front of his shins. He rolls forwards, tucking in his chin as he does *(fig 3)*. By curving the spine as in the previous exercise, the student brings his feet over his head*(fig 4)*. His arms slap out to either side and the soles of his feet kill further motion *(fig 5)*.

This exercise gives the student an accurate impression of what a rolling motion feels like. Few adults are used to thrashing about on the floor and it takes a little time to learn where the hands and feet are in relation to the mat. Only when this has been learned can the student go on to more advanced exercises.

FIG 3

FIG 4

The follow-on from this last exercise begins once more from a crouched position but this time, the student springs forwards onto his hands *(fig 6)*. The rolling motion that follows is faster than in the last exercise, bringing the heels into harder contact with the mat *(fig 7)*. The knees are well bent upon landing, so they act like shock absorbers and soak up momentum without hurting the feet. The splayed arms give stability. As with all previous exercises, the spine must be curved and the chin brought into the chest.

FIG 6

FIG 8

FIG 9

FIG 10

FIG 11

When confidence has been built up, the student can move on to performing a roll-out from a standing position. The student leans forward and extends one hand down to the floor *(fig 8)*. He then jumps forward, rolling down the curve of his arm and onto his back *(fig 9)*. By keeping his back curved, he can roll across the span of his shoulders and brake momentum by slapping down with his leading hand *(fig 10)*. The feet are brought in close to the body, in preparation for a rapid return to standing position.

Sometimes it is just not possible to roll out of a fall. When this happens, the body's impact must be cushioned by using a bent arm or leg acting as a shock absorber. The arm or leg must yield on impact, so injury is avoided. The student stands upright, with both arms extended forwards *(fig 11)*. He overbalances forwards and falls onto his hands, allowing his elbows to bend under the weight *(fig 12)*. Provided that the elbows do not simply collapse, the landing will be cushioned and injury avoided. The head must not nod forwards on landing, otherwise it could strike the floor.

FIG 12

The final fall to practise is to the side. This is done by the student laying on the floor and turning himself onto one side. He then rolls to the other shoulder, slapping down with his hand as he does so. This is repeated a number of times until he develops a feel for the movement. Then the student takes up a crouching position, and allows himself to fall to the side. As before, he slaps down with the hand closest to the floor. If the palm of this hand is turned towards the mat, the student is most unlikely to injure his funny-bone.

When the student feels confident, he can take up a standing position and deliberately unbalance himself to the side by swinging his leg out and across the front of his body *(fig 13)*. He falls to the mat, cushioning the landing with his extended arm. This yields at the shoulder joint, cushioning the force of landing. The other hand is brought protectively across the front of the face *(fig 14)*.

FIG 13

FIG 14

An Introduction to Effective Techniques

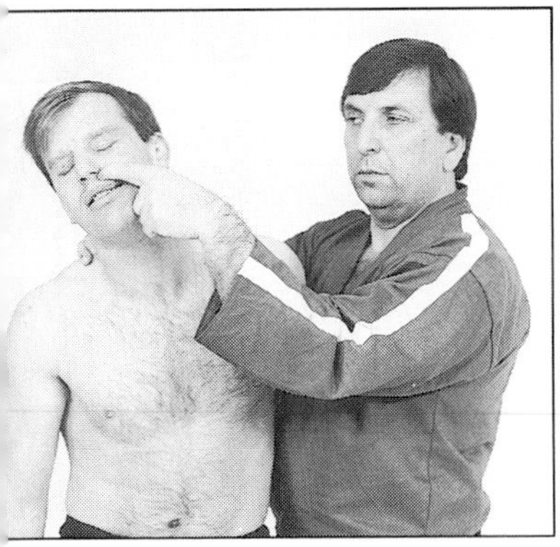

FIG 15

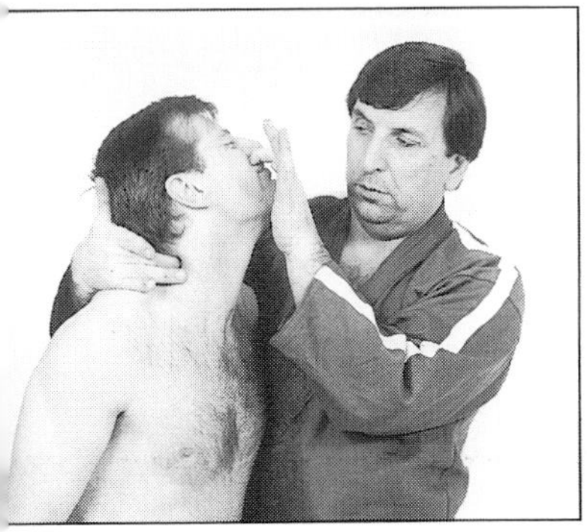

Some martial arts work on the principle that a single technique is enough to give a victory, and they train to this end. Jiu jitsu however, does not apply that principle but uses instead a succession of techniques, each one following the other in a logical sequence. It may be that the opponent is able to defeat the first technique, in which case, a second is following too quickly to allow him to take the initiative.

This strategy harks back to jiu jitsu's past, when samurai were trained to press home an unrelenting attack. All it took was one mistake in the face of this onslaught and victory was assured. Any attempt to isolate individual techniques and learn them separately poses problems because it leads to a jerky performance. The student is thinking "one-two-three" when he should be thinking of the sequence as one technique.

Nevertheless, it is possible to isolate classes of technique, if only to see how they work. A description of each follows.

The vital points

Reference to the 'vital points' has been made earlier in the book. Many are simply too dangerous to be described but others are relatively safe and are useful when used as part of escape techniques. Those selected can be applied by finger pressure alone. Alternatively, the student can make a normal fist and then push forward the middle knuckle of his index finger. This knuckle may be used with a screwing motion, in place of the fingertips.

FIG 16

Attack on pressure points gives a progressive response which allows the student to measure the amount of pain inflicted, and so avoid excessive punishment. This is therefore a good, low-key form of application.

It is not necessary to be strong in order to apply sufficient pressure, though accuracy certainly is required. The student can practise many pressure point techniques on himself but later he must learn how to use them during the to-ing and fro-ing of a simulated fight. The best way to achieve this is through partner-work.

FIG 17

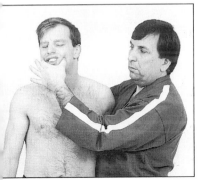

The first technique attacks a pressure point just below the nostril (fig 15), where the cartilage of the nose meets the bone of the upper jaw. Pressure at that point forces the opponent's head back. The fingertip can then be moved to the side of the nostril, where there is a second pressure point (fig 16).

The internal angle of the jaw is attacked on both sides by the thumb and index finger. These probe into the muscle bands running from the upper to the lower jaw, and press against the upper jaw (fig 17). The external angle of the jaw is attacked on one side by forcing the thumb into the hollow which is below the ear and just behind the jaw (fig 18). Pressure at this point compresses a net of nerves and causes severe pain.

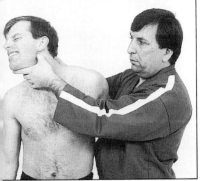

FIG 18

The throat has a number of pressure points associated with it, and the following is a safe attack provided that excessive force is not used. The thumb and fingers encircle the voice box and press inwards on either side and behind it *(fig 19)*. This causes severe pain for relatively little pressure. Lower down the neck, two bands of muscle come together just above the heads of the collarbones. At this point, there is only a thin covering of skin and superficial tissue. The index finger is driven in- and downwards, action causing feelings of pain and nausea *(fig 20)*.

The chest too, has a number of pressure points and the one selected lies just above the nipple and towards the mid-line of the body *(fig 21)*. Pressure here causes a savage, aching pain of sufficient intensity to calm even the most violent attacker. If the opponent is heavily muscled, the attack can be made with the middle knuckle of the index finger, used in a screwing motion as described above.

The opponent's grasp can be loosened by attacking the inside of his elbow joint with the fingers. The grip is stabilised by the thumb, so the opponent cannot snatch his arm away. The fingers probe inwards, just above the joint itself *(fig 22)* to where a large nerve supplies the forearm and hand. Pressure here causes a sharp pain and paralyses the lower arm.

The back of the hand can be attacked between the bones supporting the index and middle finger *(fig 23)*. Pressing this point with the index knuckle or something like a door key causes a pain sharp enough to make the opponent release his grip.

The inside of the thigh can be attacked with a pinch *(fig 24)*, or by finger pressure alone *(fig 25)*. Both of these cause a sharp pain guaranteed to make the opponent let go. The effects of the pinch can be increased by twisting the trapped flesh. An index knuckle can be used instead of the finger, to screw into the muscle.

Striking techniques
Striking techniques are used in jiu jitsu to create openings through which a lock, hold, or throw can be applied. Jiu jitsu strikes are typically fast, snapping moves that hit the target and continue on past it, or are sharply withdrawn. Many circular strikes are used because they generate a lot of power even when there is only a short distance between opponents. Their circular path gives them extra distance in which to accelerate, and makes them difficult to block.

The most common strike uses the closed fist, with the thumb locking index and middle fingers together. The thumb should not be enclosed by the fingers because this would cause it to sprain or dislocate on hard impact. The fist is held loosely until about to strike home, when it suddenly tightens. This spasm makes the fist feel a lot heavier and adds force to the impact. The thumb points upwards and only the knuckles make contact *(fig 26, see p. 36)*.

Many students experience difficulty in forming the correct fist. This is generally because they are unable to fold their fingers tightly enough into the palm. Frequent practice, assisted by pressure against the

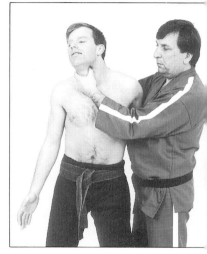
FIG 19

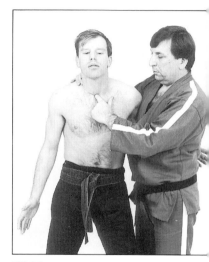
FIG 20

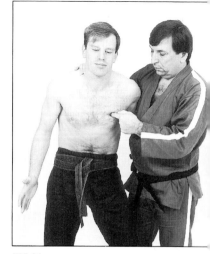
FIG 21

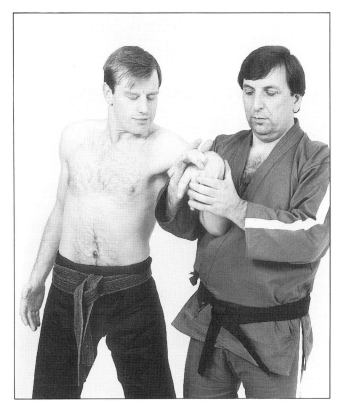

FIG 22   FIG 23

FIG 24   FIG 25

knuckles will eventually close it correctly.

Angle of the fist is also important because if the wrist is bent in any way, it will flex on impact. Punching a foam-filled pad held by a partner teaches how to align the wrist and when the student has become competent, the pad can be moved suddenly towards or away from the punch. The student should practise so he becomes equally effective when striking with either hand.

The back of the fist is used in a circular motion to strike at the side of the opponent's face *(fig 27)*. The striking action is made stronger by swinging the shoulders into the punch. The fleshy part of the fist, between the base of the little finger and wrist, is used in a circular clubbing swing to the jaw *(fig 28)*, or as a downwards-travelling blow to the back of the opponent's bowed head. Tightening the fist just prior to impact adds weight to the strike.

Semi-open fist is used where there is insuffient space to drive home a normal punch (fig 29). The fingers are folded down until their tips touch the fleshy bar at the top of the palm and the thumb is folded into the edge of the hand. Semi-open fist tightens strongly at the moment of impact. It is not so strong as the normal fist and care must be taken to avoid spraining the wrist on impact.

FIG 26

FIG

FIG 28

FIG

FIG 30

FIG 31

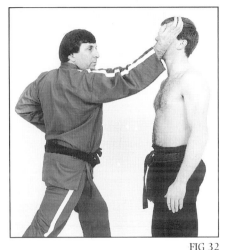

FIG 32

FIG 33

The problem of wrist-flexing is removed when palm-heel strike is used. This technique uses extended fingers but keeps the thumb pressed closely to the side of the palm. The heel of the hand is used to deliver an upwards travelling strike to the underneath of the jaw *(fig 30)*, or a curving strike to the side of the jaw *(fig 31)*. Strikes which snap the head back, or which rotate it to the side are more likely to produce a knock-out than straight punches.

The little finger-edge of the fully open hand makes a very effective weapon when used in a circular strike to the jaw *(fig 32)*, or bridge of nose *(fig 33)*. This technique is called 'knife hand'. The fingers are slightly flexed and the thumb locks across the palm. Depending upon whether it is delivered with a normal, or back-hand swing the hand rotates palm upwards, or palm downwards, respectively. The fingers stiffen on impact, so they don't rattle together. Care must be taken when using knife hand against the throat.

The thumb-side of the open hand is also used for circular strikes against the groin *(fig 34)*, or the back of the head *(fig 35)*. Contact is made just below the base of the index finger, so the thumb must be pushed inwards and out of the way. This technique is known either as 'reverse knife hand' or as 'ridge hand'.

The forearm is used for circular strikes against targets such as the throat *(fig 36)*, where a glancing blow can momentarily stun the opponent and make it easier to throw him. It is also a versatile block for deflecting a punch *(fig 37)*. When used in this way, the arm moves downwards and outwards, sweeping the punch or kick to the side of the body. In both of the examples given, the wrist should be momentarily stiffened on impact and the hand either clenched into a fist, or opened into knife hand.

FIG 34

FIG 35

FIG 36

FIG 37

FIG 38

FIG 39

Elbow is a powerful short-range circular strike or block which can be used in a variety of ways. Contact is made with the point of the elbow rather than the forearm, and delivery is such that it explodes on the target with a sharp rap, rather than as a forceful and penetrating shove. A flexible shoulder and back are essential if the strike is to develop its full potential.

Rising elbow strike *(fig 38)* uses an upwards swing of the flexed elbow into the jaw. The shoulder on the striking side swings forward, helped by the action of the opposite shoulder which pulls back strongly at the same time. The forearm is fully flexed, so the elbow is not obstructed. Both fists clench tightly at the moment of impact.

Circular elbow strike uses a swinging motion of the upper body to drive the elbow into the ribs *(fig 39)* or jaw. It is often used as part of a step forwards, when body weight adds power to the strike. For this to happen however, the elbow must make contact as forward body movement is in its final stages. Once the body has stopped advancing, this additional energy is lost. Having said that, the student must not attempt to strike while he is in the early stages of the step forwards, since this will throw his weight forwards and make him lose posture.

The unused arm is pulled back strongly and the shoulders swing in behind the strike.

Reverse elbow is useful when the opponent is standing behind, or to the side *(fig 40)*. The striking arm is pulled across the chest and then swung back into the target, aided by the action of pulling back the unused arm, and leaning into the strike. The student should further increase force by stepping into the opponent and delivering the strike as he is still moving. The hips swivel behind the elbow, to give additional power.

FIG 40

FIG 41

FIG

FIG 4

Descending elbow strike *(fig 41)* is used to attack an opponent whose head has been brought down. The striking arm is raised high into the air and then brought downwards, the elbow bending sharply as it descends. Extra force is developed if the fist is clenched tightly on impact, and if bodyweight is brought into play by bending the knees slightly. A double descending elbow strike *(fig 42)* is delivered in the same way, except that it attacks two targets simultaneously.

The elbow makes an effective and punishing block *(fig 43)* when it is swung into the path of an attacking punch. It can be used from extremely close range, perhaps with a sidestep of the front foot that takes the body to the side. This small movement is often enough to make the attacking strike miss. In such a case, the block merely functions as insurance. The elbow of the blocking arm is fully flexed and is brought into play by a swimming crawl-like overarm action. Where there is more room to move, the student plays safe and steps back, so the attack falls short. The block then acts as insurance against a chance impact arising through over-extension.

The knee is another short range weapon used to attack the groin and the thigh. It is jerked upwards and outwards as the hips push forward and the back arches. Standing on one leg close to the opponent is not recommended, so knee strike should not be used unless the student can brace himself by grasping hold of the opponent. Knee strike also should not be used if the opponent is too far away, because any attempt to reach him causes the back to over-arch. This disturbs balance and a small shove is all that is needed to sit the student down on his backside.

An instep kick uses that part of the foot between the base of the toes and the front of the ankle in a snapping attack to the groin or thigh (*fig 44*). The toes must be strongly turned down on impact, otherwise they may bend painfully. The ankle joint too must be stiffened, otherwise the foot flops about and impact force is lost. The student must be close enough to reach the target with the front of his ankle; any further away and the toes may be injured.

The kick is delivered with a snapping motion of the knee joint, as though cracking a whip. The kicking knee is accelerated up and forwards until it faces the target, then it is brought to a sudden stop. The knee joint is relaxed so when the upper leg stops, the lower leg continues on into the target. The foot is then quickly pulled back, so the opponent has no time to trap it.

The ball of the foot is a strong weapon and can be used against the opponent's stomach (*fig 45*). As with the previous example, this kick uses a snapping action of the knee joint to drive the ball of the foot into the opponent's stomach, after which it is quickly pulled back and set down.

FIG 44
FIG 45

Some students find difficulty in pulling the toes back, and so should practise this technique against a punch bag until they can perform it safely. Accurate kicking is needed if toe injuries are to be avoided. The student must always kick at an actual target, rather than in the hope of finding a target.

The little toe-edge of the foot is effective when used in a stamping action against the opponent's knee joint, but care must be taken to avoid causing injury. Stamping kick can be performed from a sideways-on position, the kicking knee being raised quite high so the foot points directly at the target. It is then driven downwards in a forceful stamp to the opponent's knee (*fig 46*). The upper body leans away in a straight line, and both arms are held in a guard position, where they can deflect chance attacks. The supporting leg swivels as the hip on the kicking side is driven into the target.

The big toe-edge of the foot is used in a scooping action to the opponent's ankle in the technique known as 'foot sweep'. This is effective when applied as the opponent is actually in the process of setting his foot down after a step. By way of contrast, foot sweep is difficult to apply when the opponent's full body weight is pressing down on the target ankle.

The heel may be used either to stamp down on the opponent's instep, or as a straight kick which thrusts directly backwards into an opponent who is standing behind. This thrust kick requires the student to lean well forwards, so it should not be attempted unless he is stable.

Locking techniques
The distinction between locking and holding techniques is one of convenience rather than strict accuracy, for there are holds which operate by locking joints and locks which operate as holds, restraining the opponent until help arrives.

FIG 46

The first joint locking techniques to consider are those which attack the fingers and thumb. These are ideal joints for attack because the associated musculature is not very strong and even the weakest person can use enough leverage to make them work. Finger locks work against the joint, forcing the opponent's finger to bend back by pushing it with the thumb, while the student's index and middle fingers are wrapped around the base.

Very often a hold can be broken by peeling back the opponent's finger and bending it backwards. The little finger is the weakest and therefore the most suitable for attack. The fingers can also be pulled apart by a two-handed attack, and the threat of dislocation this generates is a powerful deterrent.

The thumb is also attacked by forcing it against the joint (fig 47), or by making it over-flex. The latter attack is a neat little lock which can be used as a low-key restraining technique because it is unobtrusive and yet effective. The outer thumb joint is forced to bend towards the base of the thumb by pressing against it. This pressure is applied by the student's thumb, or by the palm of his hand. At the same time, his fingers grasp the opponent's hand and prevent it from being withdrawn.

The wrist is the target for a great many jiu jitsu attacks. It is easy to reach for and because it can bend in different directions, it can be attacked in many ways. The way muscles operate on and through the wrist makes it a convenient target for all students, regardless of size. Compare this situation with the shoulder, where considerable muscle strength must be overcome in order to apply a lock.

The first attack to be considered both twists and rotates the bent wrist outwards by means of pressure applied to the back of the opponent's hand (fig 48). This pressure is applied by the thumbs, which work against the fulcrum of the student's own inter-laced fingers. The thumbs actually press on pressure points, so the level of discomfort is increased.

FIG 47   FIG 48

FIG 49

First the opponent's wrist is flexed, then it is twisted so the fingers are turned towards the floor. By twisting his hips, the defender can take the opponent to the floor and hold him there. The wrist can also be twisted the opposite way, so the little finger-side of the opponent's hand is turned towards the floor *(fig 49)*. This lock is made even more effective if the opponent's elbow is lifted and bent slightly by a ridge hand applied under the elbow.

FIG 50

The wrist can be both lifted and twisted *(fig 50)*, whilst applying extra pressure with the other hand. This technique requires the opponent's elbow to be raised high. Once the lock has been applied, the opponent can be precisely controlled, and any lack of cooperation is rewarded by lifting and twisting the wrist a little more.

The wrist can be forced to bend sideways by using a double grasp with fingers interlinked on the little finger-side *(fig 51)*. The opponent's arm is fully extended and pressure is applied to his wrist until he sinks down.

The wrist can be over-flexed in the direction it normally bends *(fig 52)* by applying pressure to the opponent's knuckles. This attack works when the captured arm is straight, so the student's other hand is used to press against the opponent's elbow. A similar lock traps the opponent's elbow in the crook of the student's arm. The student flexes the opponent's wrist by pressing on the back of his hand. Increased force is applied by sliding the attacking hands further towards the opponent's fingers.

FIG 51   FIG 52

FIG 53   FIG 54

The elbow is a hinge joint and capable of moving only in two directions. In practice, the joint is attacked by over-extending it with straight arm levers. The opponent's arm is first straightened, then brought against a fulcrum, such as the student's shoulder *(fig 53)*, or thigh *(fig 54)*. Leverage is increased by moving the attacking hands further down the arm, and enough leverage can generally be exerted by just one hand.

The shoulder is a ball and socket joint and capable of a wide range of movement. Consequently it can be attacked in a variety of ways, all of which depend upon using leverage against the elbow or forearm. The greater the length of arm trapped and used, the greater the leverage on the shoulder. Shoulder locks work by forcing the joint against its limits of movement.

The first attack is a prone, double arm lever. The opponent's wrists are seized and his arms turned so that applied pressure works against the extended elbow joint. The opponent's wrists are brought together and then lifted up above his head *(fig 55)*.

FIG 55

FIG 56   FIG 57

Back-hammer *(fig 56)* is applied by passing the attacking arm under the opponent's forearm and hooking the fingers over his shoulder. This forces the opponent's bent arm up his back. By pressing down on the shoulder with both hands, the opponent can be forced to the ground and held there until help arrives *(fig 57)*.

A single arm lever works in much the same way as the double version described above. In the example shown *(fig 58)*, the opponent's arm has been drawn across his body and the other is straightened and held by pressure against the student's neck and right arm.

FIG 58

FIG 60

FIG 59

The shoulder can be attacked even when the opponent's arm is bent (*fig 59*). In this example, the opponent's left forearm is jammed in the student's armpit. The student has brought his right arm across and is applying painful leverage to the opponent's upper arm. Leverage force is increased when the student lifts his forearm. Note how the student has immobilised the opponent's other arm.

The 'figure-4 armlock' works from a bent elbow by applying force to the opponent's shoulder with interlinked arms. In the example shown (*fig 60*), the opponent's left wrist has been seized and wound into his back. The student pushes his left arm below the opponent's elbow, to link with his other hand. Leverage is increased by pressing down on the shoulder and by lifting the opponent's elbow.

The shoulder can be attacked from the front by trapping the opponent's wrist and turning it back, so the thumb points towards the floor. The student uses his left arm to push the opponent's elbow upwards, so increasing pressure on the joint (*fig 61*). If leverage is increased, the opponent topples backwards.

46

FIG 62

Holds

Strangleholds cut off the supply of blood to the brain, and prevent the opponent from breathing. They must be applied with great care, to avoid causing injury. The student must constantly monitor the opponent's response and be prepared to release instantly as he taps up.

Side stranglehold uses the forearm to bar across the opponent's throat. The student gets a firm grip of the opponent's collar, as near to the back as possible. His other hand seizes the opponent's coat *(fig 62)*. Strangles which grip the opponent's collar are often referred to as 'scarf holds'.

Front scarf hold uses a scissors action to compress both sides of the neck *(fig 63)*. It is applied by grasping the right side of the opponent's collar with the right hand, and vice versa with the left hand, so the forearms cross in front of the throat. The collar grip is tightened and the elbows bend as leverage is applied.

A variety of side scarf hold uses the free hand to force the opponent's head to the side *(fig 64)*. The student's right hand reaches down and around the opponent's throat, grasping the left side of his collar. His left hand forces the opponent's head down and to the side.

A similar hold applies the point of the student's elbow behind the opponent's ear *(fig 65)*.

FIG 65

FIG 63
FIG 64

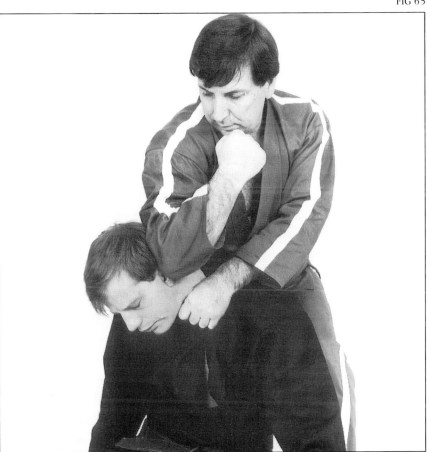

47

FIG 67

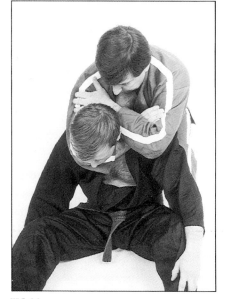

FIG 66

FIG 68

Rear strangle uses the crook of the student's elbow, so his bicep muscle and forearm press on either side of the windpipe. The fingers of the student's right hand link with the upper part of his left arm, and the opponent's head is forced forward *(fig 66)*. The student's left arm acts as a buffer, to prevent any attempts at head butt from succeeding. Standing opponents should be pulled backwards and down to the floor.

The opponent can also be held with a form of stranglehold which immobilises one of his arms *(fig 67)*. He has been taken to the floor and the student has gone under his right arm and around his neck with a headlock. The student links hands at the back of the opponent's neck and holds him firmly. To resist being thrown off by the opponent's violent struggles, the student splays his legs wide and keeps his centre of gravity low.

If the opponent wriggles onto his back, then the student lays across his chest and inserts his left arm under the opponent's neck. The opponent's left arm is wound over and under the student's leg, locking it out of harm's way. The student then uses his right hand to prevent a head butt *(fig 68)*.

The legs are used to apply a stranglehold known as the 'scissors'. The defender links his ankles together and presses inwards with his knees.

Throwing techniques

Throws can be accomplished by using locks to force the opponent to the mat. These however, will not be discussed in this section. There are many types of throws and only a few can be shown in this book. The first type unbalances the opponent by taking his centre of gravity out and beyond his feet, and then preventing him from making a corrective move.

In the illustration *(fig 69)*, the student has stepped behind the opponent's left leg with his right. By rotating his hips sharply and bringing his heel down, the defender gives the opponent's heel a powerful nudge. At the same time, he pushes the opponent diagonally backwards. The combination of these two moves unbalances the opponent backwards.

In the next example, the student 'reaps' the opponent's rear leg with a scything action *(fig 70)*. At the same time, he pushes the opponent diagonally backwards. The leg reap must be forceful and the student must throw his weight forward as he pushes, otherwise an agile opponent will turn the tables.

Throws which involve the whole body depend on getting underneath the opponent's centre of gravity and levering him over the student's back, hip, or thigh. During the course of such throws, the student generally has to turn his back on the opponent, and this can be dangerous. The opponent must first be distracted before the throw is attempted.

In the first example *(fig 71)*, the opponent has seized hold of the student's lapels. The student has quickly spun around and hooked his right arm over the opponent's right. His left arm has seized the opponent's right forearm. The defender brings his feet to a shoulder-width apart and bends his knees. Then he pulls on the opponent's right arm and draws him over his back and onto the mat.

G 69

G 70

FIG 71

FIG 72

The second throw uses both arms to draw the opponent off balance. The student steps in, turning his back on the opponent. As he does so, he takes the opponent's right upper arm in his left hand, and throws his right arm under the opponent's shoulder blade and across his back. The student steps out wide and bends his knees, whilst pulling the opponent's right arm down. At the same time, the student levers him over by using his right arm, which is wrapped around the opponent's back *(fig 72)*.

The third throw uses leverage applied to the back of the opponent's neck. The student steps forward and presses down on the opponent's neck with his left hand. At the same time, he reaches behind the opponent's back with his right arm *(fig 73)*. The student continues stepping around and forces his right hip into the opponent's stomach. He levers the opponent off balance by bending his knees and leaning forward with his upper body *(fig 74)*.

FIG 73

FIG 7

The fourth throw begins from a neck hold *(fig 75)*. The student wraps his right arm around the opponent's head and then drops onto one knee, levering the opponent over the top *(fig 76)*.

Stomach throw uses a roll back to power a strong action using the student's foot. It is best practised from a face to face position, with both partners gripping each other's lapels. The student strongly pushes the opponent backwards, causing him to resist by leaning forwards. Then the student switches attack and pulls him forwards and off balance. Keeping a tight hold of the lapels, the student rolls back onto his bottom and raises his foot, planting it firmly in the opponent's stomach. For added spice, the foot may be placed in the opponent's groin!

The opponent is lifted off his feet and brought forward, over the top of the student in a wheel-like action. By keeping hold of the opponent's lapels, he is prevented from rolling away and lands flat on his back.

FIG 75

FIG 76

Working From Close Range

FIG 77

One of the principles of jiu jitsu is maintenance of a proper distance. Yet there are occasions when this principle is difficult to apply. In recognition of this, jiu jitsu practice involves techniques which can be used from close range, i.e., when the opponent has closed and grasped hold of the defender.

The manner in which the opponent grasps the defender indicates the best response to follow. For example, if the opponent uses both hands to hold on, then the defender need not worry about an immediate punch. What he does have to consider, however, is a head butt, or attack with the knee. If the opponent uses a one handed grip, then the student must watch out for a punch from the free hand, in addition to head butt or knee strike.

FIG 78

If the opponent is standing to the rear when he grips hold, then by looking at the restraining hand, the defender will be able to tell which arm is being used and consequently, which is the safest way to turn. Supposing the restraining hand clamps on the defender's right shoulder and from the corner of his eye, the defender sees that the thumb is nearest to his neck. This tells him that the opponent has taken hold with his right hand. The best way to turn is therefore to the right, since it takes him away from the opponent's left hand. This is a small point but it is nevertheless important.

The response to a close range attack consists of a number of elements, the first of which is a distraction. This takes the form of a strike or kick. It is immediately followed by a lock, hold or throw, during which the defender may follow down to the floor and there apply a final technique. Some sequences are complex and consist of many moves.

FIG 79

Success is based upon an early and correct response to attack. In this case, the participants are standing close to each other and there is little time to respond. It is therefore a better idea to try and seize the initiative at an early stage. The defender should look at the opponent's chest area since this is where the earliest indication of attack will come, as the body is tensed to move. Some teachers recommend looking for a tell-tale narrowing of the opponent's eyes but I believe that this can be daunting and anyway, there is no record of anyone being struck by the attacker's eyeball!

Once a clear warning is perceived, the defender must act quickly and without reserve. The worst thing in the world is a half-hearted, faltering response.

Working from single hand lapel grasp
In the first sequence, the opponent grips the defender's left lapel with his right hand. Response must be immediate, otherwise the opponent's next move will be a punch to the face. Therefore as soon as the lapel is

FIG 80

seized, the defender steps back with his left foot and at the same time, strikes the opponent's chin with palm-heel. Even as the palm-heel travels to its target, the defender's left hand reaches over the top of the opponent's wrist and grasps it *(fig 77)*.

The defender presses his thumb into the back of the opponent's wrist and twists the hand free of his jacket. This action forms part of a hip rotation that brings the defender's body away from chance attack *(fig 78)*. The opponent's hand is turned so the fingers point upwards and the palm faces back towards him. The palm-heel is sharply withdrawn and the hand applied to the back of the opponent's wrist. The defender's fingers link around the front of the opponent's hand *(fig 79)*. By pushing in with the thumbs and at the same time twisting the wrist slightly, the opponent is taken to the mat.

The opponent is controlled by the wrist lock as the defender drops first to one knee, then brings that knee forwards and presses it down on the opponent's elbow and upper arm *(fig 80)*.

The student must practise this whole sequence of techniques until he can perform it smoothly and without hesitation. After the opening strike is made, the opponent must be given no time to recover the initiative. If the strike is effective, the opponent will be dazed and unable to fight back as his wrist joint is attacked. Once wrist lock is applied, it should not be released until the sequence has come to an end.

In the second sequence, the defender has responded too late and the opponent tries to punch him in the head. First priority now is to stop the punch, and this is achieved with a thrusting knife-hand block delivered as the defender steps towards the opponent. This block is made over the top of the opponent's arm. At the same time, the opponent's wrist is seized in an overhand grasp *(fig 81)*.

The defender steps around, using the rotation of his upper body to prise the opponent's fingers loose. The opponent's arm is drawn out straight and rotated, so the palm turns upwards. The opponent's fist is grasped and pushed downwards by curling the fingers of the knife-hand block around the back of his wrist *(fig 82)*. The fist is then brought underneath the opponent's other arm, which has now been fully straightened. Finally the fist is trapped beneath the opponent's straightened arm and the defender's ribcage.

Pressure is applied across the elbow joint by pressing down on the opponent's wrist. The opponent's trapped left arm functions as a fulcrum *(fig 83)*.

Although the opponent began by taking the initiative, the defender regained it by first blocking, then trapping his arms. The final held position is safe because both of the opponent's arms are tightly pinioned and any further resistance can be halted by applying pressure across the extended elbow joint.

The third sequence is slightly more complicated, involving as it does, not one but two strikes. Once again the opponent has seized the defender's lapel and thrown a punch. The defender quickly steps back and as he

FIG 81

FIG 82

FIG 83

FIG 84   FIG 85   FIG 86

does so, blocks with knife hand into the opponent's forearm *(fig 84)*. The step back is a compact movement because if it is too long, the defender's head and shoulders may be pulled forwards into the path of the punch.

Immediately following the block, the same hand is used to deliver a circular palm-heel strike to the side of the opponent's jaw *(fig 85)*. The knifehand is already close to the opponent's face and covers the additional distance in an instant. Power for this strike is provided by both hip action and the bent elbow of the preceding block. The palm-heel glances off the face, then circles around to seize the opponent's wrist in an overhand grasp *(fig 86)*.

At this point, the defender's body leans away from the opponent, so weight is taken off the front leg. This allows the defender to raise his knee, pointing the heel at the opponent's leading knee *(fig 87)*. The defender then stamp kicks to the opponent's knee with the edge of his foot whilst retaining a firm hold on his wrist *(fig 88)*. The kick is then set down and the defender rotates his hips to face the opponent.

The opponent's arm is drawn out straight and his wrist is rotated so the fingers turn upwards and outwards *(fig 89)*. The defender then steps through with his back leg while raising the attacker's arm.

The defender's forward knee is used to brace the lock, preventing the opponent from pulling away. Pressure is applied to the wrist by forcing the hand down towards the opponent's head. At the same time, the opponent's arm is lifted up and pressure applied to both elbow and shoulder joints *(fig 90)*. This lock is painful and will cause damage if applied without regard for the partner. The defender must ease pressure the instant that his partner slaps his own thigh, or taps the defender's foot.

The fourth sequence begins from the now familiar one-handed lapel grasp followed by a swinging punch. This time the defender steps away from the punch and blocks it with knife-hand *(fig 91)*. His other hand is raised to protect his face. The blocking hand loops over the top of the punch and seizes the opponent's wrist in an over-hand grasp. The punch is then taken underneath the opponent's other arm and drawn out *(fig 92)*.

54

FIG 87

FIG 88

FIG 89

FIG 90

The defender steps across with his back foot, so it comes to lie outside of the opponent's. At the same time he dips down underneath the straightened arm so the elbow comes to rest on his shoulder. Both hands then seize the opponent's hand, levering his extended arm down over the defender's shoulder. This over-extends the elbow joint and brings the opponent up onto tiptoes (fig 93).

This particular armlock clearly illustrates the effect of leverage. Only a small amount of force is needed to cause pain because downwards pressure is being exerted at the very end of the arm.

FIG 91

FIG 92

FIG 93

The fifth sequence is the final in the lapel-grasp series, and it is also the most complicated. The opponent's punch is stopped by a thrusting knife hand into the elbow as his other arm is simultaneously seized in an under-hand grasp *(fig 94)*. The fingers of the blocking knife hand close around the wrist and moving swiftly, the defender steps under the opponent's left arm *(fig 95)*.

FIG 94

For the purposes of practice, the opponent is allowed to withdraw his right arm as its grip on the defender's lapel is broken. The defender swivels his hips until his body comes to face in near enough the same direction as the opponent's. All the while he retains his wrist-hold on the opponent's punching arm, lifting it so the elbow is bent. In an effort to escape the pain of the lock, the opponent tries to punch the defender in the face with his right fist. This is blocked by a second knife-hand thrust *(fig 96)*.

By lifting and moving the captured wrist, the opponent is turned so his back is towards the defender. The latter then brings his other arm up around the front of and between the opponent's forearm and body, looping it over his shoulder in an arm entanglement *(fig 97)*. The defender releases the captured wrist and grabs the opponent's hair, dragging his head upright whilst pinioning his arm *(fig 98)*.

FIG 98

The arm entanglement is applied with the defender's hand turned palm-upwards. The reason for this will now become clear as his other hand releases the opponent's hair and whips around the front of the throat *(fig 99)*. The fingers of both hands interlace into a powerful stranglehold *(fig 100)*. Pressure must be eased the instant the opponent taps his thigh.

The defender steps back and pulls the opponent down into a sitting position whilst maintaining the hold *(fig 101)*.

Again for the purposes of practice, the stranglehold is released though the arm-entangle is still applied. The opponent is pushed down, so his head presses firmly into the mat *(fig 102)*. Finally, he is turned onto his face by lifting the arm-entangle, and trapping his head between the defender's knees *(fig 103)*.

The defender must be very careful when practising strangleholds because the carotid arteries in the opponent's throat are compressed in the vee formed by the bicep and forearm. These supply blood to the brain so pressure on them causes rapid loss of consciousness, without a great amount of struggling. This happens because breathing is not interrupted. If however, the stranglehold is applied across the windpipe, the victim struggles violently as he searches for breath.

If the stranglehold is continued to the point of unconsciousness, then brain cells die and the victim takes a long time to recover. Dead brain cells cannot be replaced, so there is a delay while uninjured cells take over their function. If a second injury to the brain occurs before healing is complete, then the resulting damage is not doubled, but multiplied several times over. For this reason, all strangleholds must stop well short of causing unconsciousness.

95

FIG 96

FIG 97

99

FIG 100

FIG 101

FIG 102

FIG 103

FIG 104   FIG 105

The next sequence is the first of a series in which the opponent grabs the defender by the wrist *(fig 104)*. The defender takes a short step backwards and circles his hand in a rising movement that both brings the opponent's arm up, and twists his wrist. With the arm held in this position, it is difficult for the opponent to throw a successful punch *(fig 105)*. It is however, an easy matter for the defender to throw a straight, jolting punch under the lifted elbow and into the opponent's jaw *(fig 106)*.

The punch is withdrawn as the defender steps quickly forwards, and the punching hand is used to seize the opponent's wrist. The defender's other hand moves around behind the opponent's extended thumb *(fig 107)*.

For the purposes of practice, the wrist/thumb hold is now changed slightly and the defender's left hand moves to the front of the captured palm, the back of the wrist forcing the opponent's fingers painfully back. The defender's other hand maintains its grip on the opponent's wrist *(fig 108)*. Quite severe pain is caused by both lifting the opponent's arm and pressing up with the back of the wrist.

FIG 108

As a further development, the defender drops his left hand and lifts the opponent's leg, whilst maintaining his attack on the wrist. Resistance to lifting the leg is countered by attacking the flesh on the inside of his thigh. The defender steps to the outside of the opponent's leg and causes him to overbalance by lifting his arm and leg still further *(fig 109)*. The wrist hold should be maintained even as the opponent falls to the ground *(fig 110)*.

FIG 107

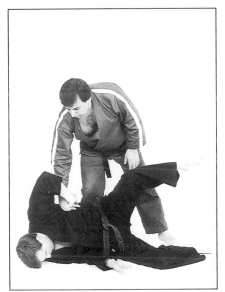

FIG 110

FIG 111

FIG 112

The second sequence also begins with the defender's wrist being grasped. This time however, he steps to the side as the opponent punches. He blocks the punch with a knife hand while simultaneously swivelling his hips, so his body faces three-quarters-on to the opponent *(fig 111)*. In the same instant, he kicks the opponent's inner thigh with his instep, to distract him *(fig 112)*.

The defender snaps his kick back and sets it down well behind his front foot, so the opponent's arm is drawn out straight. The defender breaks the grip on his wrist by raising his arm and seizing the opponent's wrist with the other hand *(fig 113)*. The opponent's wrist is then locked by turning the little finger-edge back towards him *(fig 114)*.

A snap kick with the ball of the foot to the ribs *(fig 115)* is followed by pressure on the opponent's wrist, so he is forced down to the mat. The defender then steps in close, taking his left foot over the top of the opponent's shoulder and setting it down near his chin. The wrist lock continues to be applied and the opponent's straightened arm is levered against the defender's knee. The opponent's head is forced back by the defender's foot as the other shoulder is locked against the mat *(fig 116)*.

113

FIG 114

115

FIG 116

61

The next series examines responses to double wrist grabs. As soon as the wrists are seized, the defender snap kicks into the opponent's inside thigh or groin, causing him to loosen his grip (fig 117). The defender steps diagonally outwards and uses his right hand to seize the opponent's right hand. This has already been lifted and twisted palm-upwards by the defender's left hand (fig 118). The opponent's thumb is grasped and his hand twisted around as pressure is applied to the knuckles (fig 119).

FIG 117

FIG 118

FIG 1

FIG 121

 FIG 123

The second double hand grasp sequence also uses a snap kick to the groin to distract the opponent (fig 120). The defender withdraws the kick and steps back, taking advantage of the loosened grip to reach over with an over-hand grasp to the opponent's right wrist (fig 121). The defender lifts and twists the opponent's hand, using a swivelling motion of the hips to generate power.

At the same time, his left wrist bears down on the opponent's thumb. The defender kicks a second time, using ball of foot to the opponent's ribs (fig 122). Then he steps in close to control the opponent, whilst sliding his left hand down and pressing on the opponent's upper arm. The opponent's wrist is flexed past its normal limit and slightly twisted at the same time (fig 123).

FIG 124

FIG 125

The third sequence involves a double wrist grab from the rear. This can be quickly turned into a double straight arm lever, so a fast response is called for. The defender steps to the front with his right foot, making the opponent lean slightly forwards. Then he raises his right foot and thrusts the right heel backwards and into the opponent's groin.

The third series of sequences deals with a double handed grasp of the lapels *(fig 124)*. The defender steps back and raises both hands to protect his face from a head butt *(fig 125)*. Then he kicks off his back leg, striking the opponent in the stomach with the ball of his foot *(fig 126)*. The foot is not fully pulled back, but lands in a forward position, and turned slightly so it faces the opponent.

Immediately on landing, the defender uses a circular palm-heel strike which is powered both by the energy of his moving body and by driving his shoulder behind it *(fig 127)*. The defender takes hold of the opponent's right forearm and suddenly twists his hips. The palm-heel strike continues around as the defender completely turns his back on, and winds into, the opponent *(fig 128)*. The defender now leans forward and pulls on the opponent's right arm, overbalancing him.

This throw only works effectively if the defender spins around very quickly after the strike, and pulls the opponent over his thigh. Effectiveness is lost if there is any hesitation during the wind-in, and this can leave the defender in a very precarious position.

FIG 126

FIG 127

FIG 128

FIG 129　　　　　　　　　　　　　　　　　　FIG 130

In the second sequence, the defender is seized by a double handed neck hold. Nevertheless, he takes the initiative by punching his opponent in the solar plexus. At the same time, he raises a guarding hand to ward off a chance head butt *(fig 129)*. The guard hand slides down over the opponent's face and presses into his nose, driving the head back. His other hand takes the opponent's elbow in an under-hand grasp *(fig 130)*.

The defender then steps around and back, pushing against the cartilage of the opponent's nose and lifting his arm, so he is forced down onto his side *(fig 131)*.

Quickly changing grips, the defender takes the opponent's hand from his throat, the grip having loosened during the fall. He flexes the opponent's elbow and seizes his wrist, while settling his knee into the side of the opponent's neck *(fig 132)*. Moving quickly, the defender lifts his knee and then takes his left arm under the opponent's forearm *(fig 133)*.

Rolling the opponent onto his face, the defender applies an arm-entangle, pressing down on the captured shoulder *(fig 134)*. The sequence concludes when the defender's left knee is brought forward and wedged under the captured forearm *(fig 135)*.

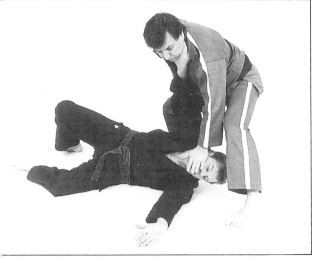

FIG 131

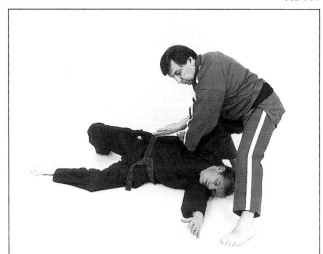

FIG 133

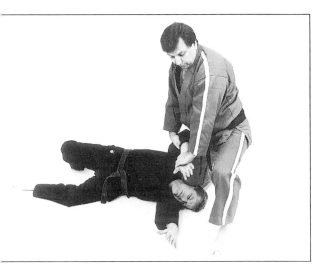

FIG 132

FIG 134

FIG 135

FIG 136

FIG 137

The next series deals with grasping attacks from the rear, the first with a single hand *(fig 136)*. The defender steps sharply forwards, pulling the opponent off balance as he does so. The opponent throws a punch but this is blocked by the defender's forearm, while his other hand guards the face *(fig 137)*. Once the punch is stopped, it is seized by the guarding hand as the other pulls back *(fig 138)*, in preparation to use a back elbow *(fig 139)*. This is a very powerful strike which makes use of the body's rotation and forward movement.

The defender slides his elbow under the opponent's left arm in a circular motion, and raises it high *(fig 140)*. This action traps the opponent's arm against the back of the defender's neck and levers him down. His other arm is pulled straight across the front of the defender's thigh *(fig 141)*.

FIG 138

FIG 139

FIG 140

FIG 141

FIG 142

FIG 143

The second sequence starts in much the same way except this time, the defender blocks with a knife hand *(fig 142)*. The spent punch is seized in the defender's left hand as the right coils back *(fig 143)*, in preparation for a back fist strike to the side of the opponent's jaw *(fig 144)*. The striking arm is then raised high *(fig 145)* and is brought sharply down in a descending elbow strike to the opponent's left arm *(fig 146)*.

The striking arm then loops under the opponent's and traps it in the defender's armpit. The opponent's right arm is brought across his body as the defender turns sideways, and forces the trapped shoulder to rotate inwards. Only slight pressure is needed to bring the opponent to his toes *(fig 147)*.

FIG 144

FIG 145

FIG 146

FIG 147

71

FIG 148   FIG 149   FIG 150

The third sequence begins with a back-hammer hold applied from the rear. This is a painful technique during which the bent arm is forced up the back. A strong opponent can inflict a lot of pain, so it is important to counter immediately.

The defender steps forward, pulling the opponent off balance. As he does this, he attacks the opponent's ribs with a back fist strike *(fig 148)*. The opponent might well try to use his knee, or to kick from this position. If this happens, then the defender thrusts down with the edge of his hand, and prevents the kick from developing *(fig 149)*.

The defender ducks quickly under the opponent's arm, maintaining an effective guard with his untrapped hand *(fig 150)*. Completing the step through, the opponent's grip is reversed. The defender's left arm is inserted below the opponent's bent elbow, and grips the other wrist to make a figure-4 armlock *(fig 151)*. The defender then steps around, so his right foot comes to lie in front of the opponent's *(fig 152)*.

The defender falls backwards while maintaining the armlock, and pulls the opponent down with him *(fig 153)*. The opponent is obliged to make a full roll and ends up laying on his back, with his arm still pinioned *(fig 154)*. The defender brings his left foot over in a snapping kick to the groin *(fig 155)* and on the way back, hooks it around his other ankle to make a neck scissors *(fig 156)*. Care must be taken to avoid applying too much pressure across the throat.

This sequence illustrates the fact that an opponent must always be watched closely to prevent him from re-taking the initiative. If the defender is not alert to the possibility of further attack, then a surprise kick or punch from the opponent can soon turn the tables.

FIG 151

FIG 152

FIG 154

FIG 156

FIG 157

FIG 158

FIG 159

FIG 160

The next sequence begins from a back hammer hold and rear collar grasp. The defender steps forward and performs back fist to the opponent's ribs, whilst grasping his right hand *(fig 157)*. The defender steps around with his rear foot, so it comes to lie outside of the opponent's *(fig 158)*. Then he twists his hips sharply and raises the opponent's right hand, flexing his arm at the elbow *(fig 159)*. The defender then inserts his left arm underneath the opponent's and links with his right wrist, to make a figure-4 armlock *(fig 160)*.

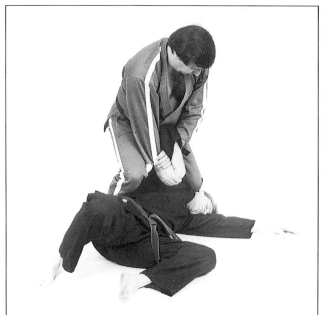

FIG 161

FIG 162

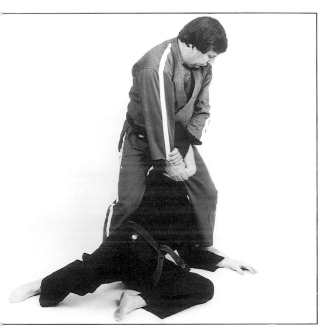

FIG 163

FIG 164

The defender twists his hips still further whilst maintaining the lock. The pain this causes makes it easy to throw the opponent *(fig 161)*, and he lands at the defender's feet *(fig 162)*. The defender then steps across and lifts the opponent by his flexed wrist *(fig 163)*. Care must be taken to avoid fracturing it. Finally, the defender kneels astride the opponent, settling his body weight on the latter's left arm *(fig 164)*.

Mid-range Techniques

This chapter will consider the strategy and techniques used when participants are at the correct distance from each other, and both have freedom of movement. Are they close enough together for the opponent simply to reach forward and grab the defender, or must he first take a step forwards? Skilled jiu jitsu practitioners can respond appropriately from any distance but beginners need more time in which to think, and to select an appropriate response. Beginners therefore need to stand farther apart than trained martial artists.

Distance can be corrected in a number of ways. The first involves a short initial movement of the leading foot, then the rear foot is brought up. Neither foot is lifted up, both slide smoothly over the mat. Whenever the front moves, the back foot moves an equal distance, so the stance neither shortens nor stretches out. Larger distances can be covered by lunging forwards (or backwards) on the rear foot, always ensuring that the rear foot moves an equal distance.

The defender always looks at the opponent's chest. As soon as the opponent steps forward, the defender can respond in one of three ways. Firstly he can take a step back, so the opponent's attack is out of range. This presents a slight problem insofar as the opponent needs simply step forward once more. Ultimately, the person moving forwards is faster than the one retreating backwards. Therefore the step back is best used once, after which another response should be made. The step back can be thought of as a make-safe move, during which a response can be formulated.

The defender can also step forwards, into the attack. This is not as suicidal as it sounds because all techniques are aimed at a specific target and when that target is moved – even by a small amount – they fail. By stepping into an attack, the opponent's techniques are given insufficient distance over which to build up force. His punch or kick is only just beginning, or he has just started to reach forward. He has committed himself to an attack and is then confused because the object of attack, attacks him!

Having said that, it is pointless for the defender to step blindly into an attack if he doesn't know what he is going to do when he closes range. Furthermore, the step forward must not be made direct into the path of a straight punch to the face! The student must always maintain a safe guard – especially when stepping forwards.

Stepping to the side is an effective form of avoidance because although it removes the defender from the direct line of attack, it still leaves him close enough to respond quickly. Stepping to the side can be done with either the leading, or the rear foot. Front foot side step is followed by a rotation of the hips, so the student's body turns through 90 degrees.

This is normally enough to make a technique miss, and even if it isn't, the body's rotation will make it glance off harmlessly. The amount of side step actually taken determines how far the student withdraws from the path of the attack. Obviously this should be as little as is consistent with safety, since the time lag for delivering a response is then reduced. Beginners often step so far to the side that they can't reach the opponent!

The rear leg too can be used to step diagonally out and back. The side step is made with the ball of the foot, then the hips twist away from the direction of attack, withdrawing the leading leg. A guard must be maintained throughout the evasion.

These evasions must be practised regularly until they can be performed smoothly and without hesitation. As skill improves, the student will learn to delay the evasion until the last instant, so it goes undetected. Too early a move allows the opponent to adjust his attack.

Timing is also a factor to be considered when training at middle distance. For example, the opponent may decide to throw a punch. This begins from a slow speed and accelerates sharply towards the anticipated point of contact. When the punch misses, speed falls rapidly as it is brought to a stop. If the opponent makes a strong attack, the amount of body involvement will make it slow to recover.

It therefore follows that a response which is made just as the opponent begins a punch, or just after the punch has missed, will have a better chance of being successful. Skilled jiu jitsu practitioners see the opponent's technique at an early stage and close quickly. Less experienced students are advised to make-safe and respond immediately after the attack has missed.

The time-lag between an attack missing and its recovery is very short, so a response must begin the instant the attack is seen to have missed. This harks back to the previous section and reinforces the need to remain close to, but safe from, the opponent at all times.

Stance is important because the student who stands square-on to his opponent will be presenting a wide area of target. Contrast this with the student who stands with body turned slightly away. If his left leg leads, then the left arm is extended over it. The right hand is held in front of the chest, where it can either block an attack, or launch a counter-attack. Both hands are curled into semi-open fists, so the fingers are difficult to seize hold of.

Length of stance is not fixed, though as a general rule, it should not be so long as to make movement slow, nor so high that the student is easily bowled over by a strong advance. The stance should include a little side step, so the front and rear feet are not in line. Too much sidestep opens the groin to attack and too little leads to an unstable stance.

FIG 165

FIG 166

FIG 167

The first series begins from a fighting distance where the backs of the wrists are in contact *(fig 165)*. The opponent moves forwards and makes a strong punch. Immediately the defender swivels his hips and moves his body away. At the same time he blocks with right knife hand whilst guarding his face with the left *(fig 166)*. The opponent's punch is seized with the left hand *(fig 167)* and a knife-strike made to the ribs *(fig 168)*.

After impact, the knife hand is rammed upwards and underneath the opponent's armpit. Then the opponent's right arm is successively drawn out straight, pushed down *(fig 169)*, folded back and then trapped with the defender's right hand. The defender's left hand braces the lock and prevents the arm from breaking free by pressing upwards against the opponent's elbow *(fig 170)*.

FIG 168

FIG 169

FIG 170

FIG 171

FIG 172

In the second sequence, the opponent has thrown a straight punch and this is blocked by palm-heel *(fig 171)*. The defender quickly responds with a straight punch to the opponent's ribs before the latter has a chance to withdraw his arm *(fig 172)*. The defender lunges forward off his rear foot, closing distance and using his right hand to push the opponent's right arm across his chest. At the same time, the defender's left arm whips around the back of the opponent's neck *(fig 173)* and seizes his right arm at the elbow *(fig 174)*. The defender then jams the opponent's head against his chest and attacks it with his elbow *(fig 175)*.

FIG 173

FIG 174

FIG 175

The third sequence begins with the opponent throwing a straight punch. This is deflected by a downwards-travelling circular knife block. In the same instant, the opponent's throat is attacked with half-open fist *(fig 176)*. The fist passes around and behind the opponent's neck, pulling his head down. At the same time, his right arm is forced upwards and trapped against the defender's left shoulder *(fig 177)*. The defender then steps past the opponent's head and seizes his free arm, pulling it upwards *(fig 178)*.

The sequence concludes with the defender kneeling down and trapping the opponent's head. The opponent's left arm is locked against the defender's right knee, so that both arms are immobilized *(fig 179)*.

FIG 176

FIG 177

FIG 178

FIG 179

The fourth sequence opens with a large side step to avoid the opponent's powerful, lunging punch. For added insurance, the evasion is reinforced with a thrusting knife hand block *(fig 180)*. Because the defender has stepped wide, he can kick to the opponent's kidneys, using the ball of his foot for extra penetration *(fig 181)*.

The kicking foot is set down in a forward position and the defender leans away, holding his right arm up as a guard. He seizes the opponent's punch with his left hand *(fig 182)* and delivers a reverse elbow into the opponent's face *(fig 183)*. Then he loops his arm around the opponent's throat *(fig 184)*. All the while, the opponent's left arm remains tightly gripped in the defender's left hand.

The defender drops to his knee and takes the opponent with him *(fig 185)*. The opponent's straight arm is levered across the defender's left knee and his head is forced backwards *(fig 186)*.

This is an extremely dangerous technique, and must be practised with caution. If the head is forced back too far, the opponent's neck can be broken!

FIG 180

FIG 181

FIG 182

FIG 183

FIG 184

FIG 185

FIG 186

FIG 187

FIG 188

FIG 189

FIG 190

The fifth sequence opens with a strong straight punch from the opponent. This is sidestepped and the defender remains close enough to block with his rear hand, choosing a circular action which curls across the opponent's hand in an overhand grasp *(fig 187)*. The captured wrist is rotated so the fingers point straight up. Note the defender's face guard *(fig 188)*. The defender then uses the ball of his foot to kick to the opponent's solar plexus *(fig 189)*. This acts as a distraction while a second lock is applied.

FIG 191

FIG 192

FIG 193

FIG 194

The defender closes distance and brings his left arm underneath the opponent's elbow. Lifting the elbow causes pain *(fig 190)* and makes it easy to take the opponent down onto his knee *(fig 191)*. The defender reaches around with his left hand and takes the fingers of the trapped wrist, all the while keeping the opponent's arm raised *(fig 192)*. If the elbow is allowed to drop, the hold loses its effectiveness.

The opponent's arm is forced down and brought around into a straight arm lever. It is then locked by pressing down on the shoulder and by wedging the arm against the defender's left thigh *(figs 193 and 194)*.

FIG 195

FIG 196

In the sixth sequence, the defender steps to the side with his rear leg and twists his hips away. He blocks the opponent's punch with a circling palm *(fig 195)* and then twists back to face the opponent, striking with his right forearm as he does so *(fig 196)*. The defender's other hand remains in control of the opponent's right arm. The right arm loops around the opponent's neck and makes contact with the defender's left arm. The hands join up and make an effective lock *(fig 197)* with which the opponent can be taken to the floor *(fig 198)*. The defender splays his legs wide and sinks his body low, to avoid being thrown off by the opponent's struggles.

FIG 197

FIG 198

FIG 199   FIG 200   FIG

FIG 2

FIG 2

In the seventh sequence, the defender steps well to the side with his front foot and twists his hips away from the attack. He then blocks the opponent's punch with a circling palm, performed by the rear hand. The other remains in a guard position near the face *(fig 199)*. The punch is seized in an overhand grasp and the wrist both lifted and twisted so the fingers point upwards. By way of distraction, the defender lifts his right knee and drives the edge of his foot into the opponent's knee *(fig 200)*.

The kicking foot is set down in a forward position and the opponent's wrist is lowered. The defender's right hand loops up under the opponent's elbow, where it serves as a block against a chance punch *(fig 201)*. The opponent's right arm is then straightened and the defender withdraws his left hand, bringing it over the top, and then down onto the opponent's arm *(fig 202)*.

The opponent's right wrist is released and his arm is brought around and up behind his back. The defender's left arm slips under the opponent's forearm and over his shoulder *(fig 203)*, to make an arm entanglement. The defender maintains this hold and takes the opponent face down to the mat, applying the lock with one hand and pressing the opponent's head down with the other *(fig 204)*.

The defender lunges forward over the opponent's back *(fig 205)*, trapping his right arm in the process. Then he brings his right arm around the back of the opponent's neck *(fig 206)* and levers him onto his back. The defender kneels on the opponent's right hand and forces his left arm down to the mat *(fig 207)*. Whilst maintaining the grip on the opponent's left wrist, the defender forces his left arm down behind the opponent's neck *(fig 208)*. The opponent's left arm is then fed under the defender's flexed left knee and locked. Meanwhile the defender's right hand covers the opponent's face to prevent a chance head butt *(fig 209)*.

FIG 204

FIG 205

FIG 206

FIG 207

FIG 208

FIG 209

The eighth sequence uses a front foot side step and palm-heel block to the opponent's punch (fig 210). The block develops into a push which takes the punching arm down (fig 211) and exposes the opponent's neck to a reverse knife hand strike (fig 212). The defender then brings his right leg forward and drives it behind the opponent's leading leg. At the same time, he thrusts with both hands against the opponent's chest, forcing him diagonally backwards and off balance (fig 213).

FIG 210

FIG 211

FIG 212

FIG 2

FIG 214

FIG 215

FIG 216

FIG 217

The ninth sequence takes the attacker's punch on to the front guard hand and draws it down and forwards. The other hand guards the defender's face from the opponent's left fist. The degree of evasion employed is very slight, consisting merely of a slight hip twist to bring the right hand forwards (*fig 214*). This places it in a good position for a fast knife hand strike to the opponent's neck (*fig 215*). The defender's left hand remains in contact with the opponent's right arm.

The defender steps up with his right leg, placing it behind the opponent's leading leg (*fig 216*) and sweeping him diagonally backwards to the floor. The defender maintains an effective guard throughout (*fig 217*).

FIG 218

FIG 219

The tenth sequence uses a thrusting knife hand block to deflect a punch *(fig 218)*. The opponent's right wrist is then seized in an overhand grip. At the same time, the defender's right hip drives forwards and his right arm reaches past the opponent's right shoulder *(fig 219)*. The defender steps quickly forward, placing his right leg behind the opponent's leading leg *(fig 220)*. By turning his hips, the defender unbalances the opponent, allowing him to fall to the mat without releasing the wrist hold *(fig 221)*. The defender then steps over the attacker, bringing his left leg around the back of the opponent's pinioned right arm and setting the heel down on the attacker's left arm *(fig 222)*.

FIG 220

FIG 221

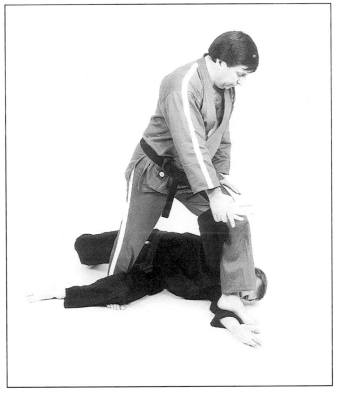

FIG 222

FIG 223

FIG 224

FIG 225

FIG 2

The eleventh sequence uses a knife hand block to deflect the opponent's punch *(fig 223)*. The defender quickly follows up with a ridge hand strike to the side of the opponent's neck *(fig 224)*. This action takes weight off the rear foot, so it can be brought through and used to attack the opponent's kidneys *(fig 225)*. The leg is first straightened and then hooked back into the opponent's right leg. In the same instant he is pushed backwards *(fig 226)* off balance. The opponent falls to the mat but remains pinioned by his right arm. This is levered back over the defender's knee *(fig 227)* and a punch to the face concludes the sequence *(fig 228)*.

The defender's reverse knife hand must follow quickly after knife block, otherwise the opponent can counter with his right hand.

FIG 227

FIG 228

FIG 229

FIG 230

The next sequence uses a powerful hiptwist to bring the defender's rear hand forward into a palm-heel strike. At the same time, the defender deflects the opponent's punch with a knife block *(fig 229)*. The attacking fist is pushed down as the defender continues turning and sliding his right arm under the opponent's shoulders *(fig 230)*.

The defender turns fully and bends his knees, dropping under the opponent's centre of gravity. At the same time, he pulls down on the opponent's right arm and begins to lift with his right arm *(fig 231)*. The defender straightens his legs and continues the lift and pull-over *(fig 232)*, dumping the opponent onto his back. The opponent's right arm remains trapped and upon landing, it is straightened out and locked with a figure-4 hold. The defender's knee presses into the back of the opponent's head *(fig 233)*.

FIG 232

FIG 233

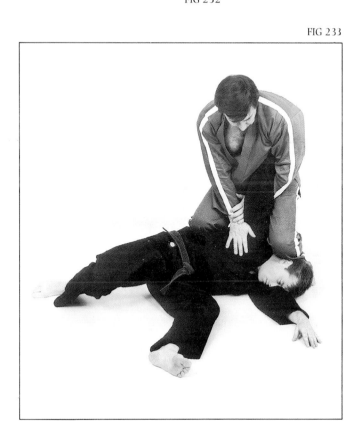

FIG 234

FIG 235

In the next sequence, the defender takes a full step back and deflects the opponent's punch with his right forearm. He seizes the opponent's punch with his left hand *(fig 234)* and strikes back into the opponent's jaw with a back fist. The opponent's punching arm is then pulled down and drawn out *(fig 235)*. The defender twists his hips fully, whilst pulling down on the opponent's right arm and lifting him by means of an arm wrapped around his back *(fig 236)*. This combination of lifting and pulling takes the opponent over the defender's hip and down onto the floor, where he remains held by a straight armlock *(fig 237)*.

The defender steps over and brings his leg behind the opponent's head, wedging his foot under the opponent's left arm *(fig 238)*. By forcing his leg straight, the defender can exert pressure on the back of the opponent's neck. Great care must be taken to avoid causing injury with this last technique.

FIG 237

FIG 238

FIG 239

FIG 240

FIG 241

FIG 242

The next sequence uses knife block to deflect the opponent's straight punch *(fig 239)*. The defender steps through with his rear foot, pushing back the opponent's punching arm as he does so *(fig 240)*. He withdraws his right arm and delivers an elbow strike to the opponent's ribs as his forward motion is coming to a stop *(fig 241)*. The defender hooks his right arm up behind the opponent's left to act as the fulcrum of a straight arm lever *(fig 242)*. Then he turns and drops below the opponent's centre of gravity, bearing down on the opponent's straightened arm *(fig 243)*, and throwing him to the mat.

FIG 243

FIG 244

FIG 245

FIG 246

FIG 247

FIG 248

The forearm is used with an action like the windscreen wiper of a car to block the opponent's next punch *(fig 244)*. The defender then uses this same hand for a glancing palm-heel strike across the opponent's jaw *(fig 245)*. The strike carries on past, then loops back around the side of the opponent's head *(fig 246)*. The defender brings his rear leg forward and twists his hips, so he faces the same way as the opponent *(fig 247)*. His right arm goes around the opponent's back. The defender then steps through, bringing both feet close together and drawing the opponent over his hip *(fig 248)* and down onto the floor.

FIG 249

FIG 250

FIG 251

FIG 252

FIG 253

FIG 254

The next sequence begins with a front foot side step that takes the defender away from the opponent's straight punch. For added insurance, the opponent's punching arm is deflected by a thrusting knife block (*fig 249*). The other hand serves as a guard. The opponent is turned by pushing against his punching arm, and his attempted back fist with the left hand is stopped by a palm-heel block (*fig 250*).

The opponent is then jolted forwards off balance by a head butt to his back (*fig 251*). Before he can recover, the defender drops down and gathers both ankles (*fig 252*), jerking them back and dumping the opponent onto his face (*fig 253*). The defender skips forward to deliver a heel kick to the back of the opponent's head (*fig 254*). Then he picks up the opponent's arms and levers them forwards (*fig 255*). The defender drops to his right knee, pinioning the opponent's right arm with a wrist hold and his left with a straight arm lever (*fig 256*). The defender's other leg is brought around and wedged behind the opponent's neck (*fig 257*).

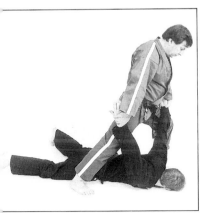

FIG 255   FIG 256   FIG 257

FIG 258   FIG 259   FIG 260

In the final sequence, the defender deflects a punch with a forearm block delivered from a sideways-on position *(fig 258)*. The block is withdrawn and the same arm used to deliver a back elbow strike to the opponent's ribs *(fig 259)*. The defender then steps across with his left leg, raising his right arm *(fig 260)* in preparation for a back elbow strike *(fig 261)*. The hips turn behind the strike to make it more powerful. The defender then reaches over and takes the opponent by the back of his neck *(fig 262)*. By dropping onto his right knee and pulling with his right arm, the defender topples the opponent forward onto the mat *(fig 263)*.

As the opponent lands, his left arm is trapped by the defender's leg *(fig 264)*. The defender's left arm whips around the opponent's throat whilst the right forces his head down *(fig 265)*.

FIG 261

FIG 262

FIG 263

FIG 264

FIG 265

Groundwork Techniques

No matter how skilled the participants, one or both may end up rolling about on the mat as a result of being thrown, tripped, or simply losing their balance. The martial artist laying prone on the mat has two objectives; the first is to escape, and the second is to defeat the opponent. No engagement is over until one of the participants submits, so it is therefore essential that a part of the syllabus is devoted to groundwork.

Groundwork is all close range work and there is little possibility for effective striking techniques, though attacks on pressure points remain feasible. Response is essentially restricted to escape techniques, holds and locks.

The weaker martial artist prone on the mat is in a poor position because he cannot maintain an effective distance from the stronger opponent, and neither can he use evasion in the face of attack. Skill and determination are the only plus factors on his side. For his part, the opponent will attempt to apply a hold or a lock, whilst resisting the defender's attempts to counter. In terms of general strategy, it is always better to try and get on top, because body weight can then be used to help pin the opponent down. Regular groundwork training is essential because it builds the ability to think and act in a coordinated manner in a prone situation.

The first requirement of groundwork is an effective guard, so the defender must roll onto his side, facing the opponent. His upper knee is bent and closes the groin, his elbows protect the stomach and chest, and his fore-arms protect the face. As the opponent moves, the defender does too, paddling himself around with his lower foot.

The defender's feet make useful weapons and with a little practice, one can be hooked around the opponent's ankle whilst the other lashes out at his knee. Alternatively, the defender can throw himself into the opponent's shins, trap them, and cause him to fall over backwards. The defender then rolls up and over his legs, lashing out into his groin or face with an elbow or hammer fist.

If the defender manages to get on top, then he should try to stay there by spreading his feet as wide as possible. For maximum stability, he should sit on the ground whilst maintaining a tight hold. It is easier to squirm out from underneath the opponent if he is not firmly anchored.

Any loose limbs should be seized and locked. Strangleholds are effective when used in a prone position, though the student must ensure that he is stable as he applies them. Rear strangle is perhaps the most effective. Scissors work well because they are applied by the legs while the body lies on the mat. The arms can either be used to stabilise the defender, or to apply an arm lever.

Necklocks are dangerous and should be used with caution. This applies especially to the lock illustrated (*fig 266*). A side headlock is safer, and is made more effective if the opponent's arm is also trapped *(fig 267)*. Side pinion is both safe and effective because it locks the head in a natural position *(fig 268)*.

FIG 267

FIG 268

Escape techniques are equally important and two examples showing escape from prone strangle are included. In the first sequence, the opponent kneels inside the defender's legs *fig 269)*. The defender uses left palm-heel in a glancing blow across the opponent's face, and then seizes his right wrist in an over hand grasp. At the same time, he brings his right leg up, placing the sole of his foot against the opponent's knee *fig 270)*.

Then several things happen at once. The defender pushes the opponent's knee down and simultaneously twists to the right. This dislodges the

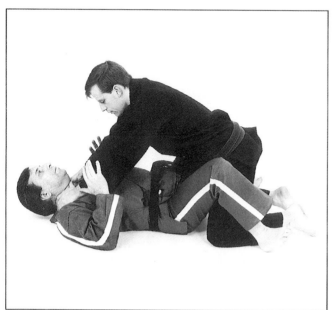

FIG 269

FIG 270

FIG 271

FIG 2

opponent, who collapses onto his chest, leaving his right wrist still trapped *fig 271*). Then the defender swings his right foot over and wedges it under the opponent's chin *fig 272*). The defender rolls up onto his right knee, keeping the trapped right arm straight and stepping firmly on the opponent's left arm (*fig 273*).

The opponent's arm is brought back and trapped between the defender's thigh and ribs (*fig 274*). By bringing his right knee down, the defender forces the opponent's right arm to the mat (*fig 275*). The defender needs only to lean forwards to increase pressure on the arm (*fig 276*).

FIG 273

FIG 274

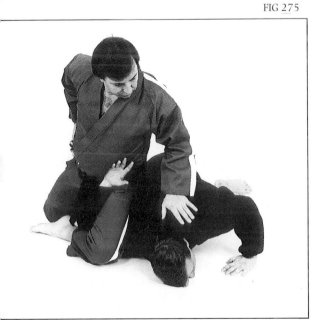

FIG 275

FIG 276

The second sequence begins in a similar way. The defender thrusts his right arm up and simultaneously seizes the opponent's right wrist with his left hand. He brings his right knee up to force the opponent away and to lessen his grip (*fig 277*). Then he brings his left leg up and hooks the opponent's head (*fig 278*), forcing it down to the mat. The defender draws out the opponent's arm and straightens it against his right thigh (*fig 279*).

Then the defender drops his left leg and brings the opponent's arm across and over his left thigh (*fig 280*). He quickly swings his right leg over and wedges the knee behind the opponent's head, and the instep around his elbow (*fig 281*).

FIG 277

FIG 2

FIG 279

FIG 2

FIG 281

Jiu Jitsu and Self Defence

Surprisingly perhaps, not all martial arts are suitable for using as self defence. Over many years, some became more interested in sporting applications, altering their techniques to give a better chance of winning, according to whatever artificial rules were imposed. Other martial arts changed their priority from defeating an opponent, to defeating one's own ego. In many cases, this meant the adoption of ritual, and technique practice for technique's sake. Yet other martial arts have remained frozen in a traditional mould, training their students to become expert swordsmen in a world where no one now carries swords.

Jiu jitsu has avoided all these changes and remains a pragmatic system of self defence, whether used against an opponent armed with a spear, or against one brandishing a pistol.

It is worth noting that many martial arts represent single lines of development. An impact-based system may restrict its syllabus to striking techniques, and ignore the obvious benefits of locks, holds and throws. Certainly that system can become highly specialised and effective, but regrettably only within a narrow range of application.

By way of comparison, jiu jitsu covers a whole range of techniques within its syllabus, including striking as well as grappling. This is the case because jiu jitsu never abandoned the teachings of the many traditional ryu which collectively make it up.

Self defence is a method of avoiding a situation where there is a risk of actual attack by one or more opponents. Without doubt, the best self defence system is one which is based upon the principles of observation, awareness, and evaluation. It is surely much better to avoid trouble in the first instance, than to deal with it once it has arisen. No matter how sophisticated, any type of physical response is unsatisfactory and should be used only when all else fails.

The self defence benefits conferred by jiu jitsu training increase with the number of years spent in practice. Unfortunately there is no quick or easy answer.

Jiu jitsu's wide syllabus provides enough techniques to meet every eventuality, and every size and shape of student. The techniques used are based upon realistic attacks and each has the widest possible application. The jiu jitsu training method teaches how to use these techniques in a progressive manner, with each lesson recapping previous techniques rather than constantly introducing new material. Regardless of how individual the attack is, it can nevertheless be steered into a familiar pathway.

Jiu jitsu techniques are organised into a progressive syllabus which means that the simpler ones are taught first. When adequate skill and coordination have been developed, more advanced techniques are introduced, and so on until the student has a wide grasp of technique and its application. A systematic approach such as that described aids learning and builds confidence. Jiu jitsu techniques actually flow into each other, so they have to be learned as one. This may seem difficult at first, but it obviates serious problems arising from the faltering step-by-step approach of more simple systems.

The philosophy of jiu jitsu training instils a sense of realism amongst the participants. This removes the unwarranted self-confidence that comes from working/dealing with cooperative opponents. Jiu jitsu always tries to be as realistic as possible.

It has been claimed that any response to an attack is likely to result in an escalation of violence. Certainly a half-hearted response may have this effect, so once a decision is made to make a physical response, then 100% effort must be given. In any self defence situation, the will to win counts for more than technical ability.

In terms of self defence, jiu jitsu offers:

    (a)   a theoretical approach to self defence in terms of observation, avoidance, security measures, mental attitude and legal implications;

    (b)   a basic practical approach which looks at posture, distancing, line, body weapons, force, vulnerable targets and blocks;

    (c)   an advanced practical using a modular system to deal with realistic attacks through an ascending series of techniques.

Referring firstly to the theoretical section, jiu jitsu teaches the student how to use powers of observation to detect areas of potential danger. This method of training is based upon the precepts of the classical Japanese warrior who lived in dangerous times. It operates in the same way that other everyday actions do. No one consciously thinks through the chain of physical actions which lead to opening a door. The habit has been learned and stored. Observation too becomes an unconscious habit.

Observation leads naturally on to personal safety and jiu jitsu teaches how to respond to various attack situations which may be encountered in the home, or on public transport etc. Hand in hand with observation is avoidance; how to minimise the risk perceived. In practical terms, this can be extended to knowing where to sit on a bus or train.

The progressive nature of jiu jitsu techniques makes it possible to apply them with control. Contrast this with the all-or-nothing response of the purely impact-based systems. This factor is particularly important from a legal point of view since the law states that only sufficient force as is necessary to neutralise an attack, is lawful. Usage of excessive force makes the victim liable to legal action.

Within the wide jiu jitsu syllabus are techniques suitable for every self defence occasion, that is why the art is used by police officers, prison officers, security personnel and members of the armed services. The prison officer who uses an impact-based martial art to control a prisoner will soon find himself in court!

Jiu jitsu based theories on timing teach when to respond to an attack and conversely, when not to. Indeed, there are self defence situations where a practical response is impossible. In such cases, the best thing to do is to wait for an opportunity.

Since attacks are normally aimed at a target, it follows that if that target is moved, the attack may miss. This describes the dual concepts of distancing and evasion, both of which are integral to jiu jitsu practice. In many cases, only a small movement is required to make an attack miss completely. Training teaches how to move by the smallest safe distance in the right direction, so the student can respond quickly and without hesitation.

Blocking techniques reinforce the evasion mentioned above. A block meets the opponent's attack at an angle, redirecting its force harmlessly away. Often this has spectacular results.

Jiu jitsu teaches how to generate force in strikes and grapples by using a relaxed technique delivery, which does not require large muscles for it to be effective. Wherever possible, short distance circular strikes are used because these begin close to the target and their circular path makes them difficult to block. In conjunction with strikes, jiu jitsu makes use of the body's pressure points to generate a large effect from a small effort.

The jiu jitsu syllabus includes both striking techniques and holds, locks and throws. Strikes are quicker to learn but grapples are more controllable. There is therefore a fairly immediate short term self defence benefit, and a greater but more gradual long term benefit from jiu jitsu practice.

The scientific principles of leverage ensure that a small person can subdue a larger opponent and to help achieve this, jiu jitsu uses a strike as an opening distraction to gain time during which to apply the grapple. The opponent's response must be allowed for as the two techniques link together and if it is unsuitable, then the provision exists to change or even abort the planned counter attack.

In this book, I have considered the application of jiu jitsu techniques in three situations. The first situation arises when, despite the student's usage of evasion and distance, the opponent has closed and seized hold. The second situation arises when the attacker is successfully kept at a safe distance, and the third arises when both participants have fallen to the floor. This last situation is very important because nearly all self defence involves some scrabbling about on the floor. In such circumstances, the student must remain able to think and act decisively.

Concerning Safety

Before students begin training in jiu jitsu, it is as well if they consider and take on board, the rules of safe practice. First of all, are the students fit enough to train? When did they last take any form of physical exercise? If a student is over forty years of age and has previously led an inactive life, then it is best if he sees the doctor before training, and gets a clean bill of health. Unaccustomed hard training has an unfortunate habit of showing up physical weaknesses, often with unpleasant results.

Hay fever, diabetes and asthma are no bar to training, but medication must always be kept within easy reach. One jiu jitsu coach in my Association asks students undergoing drug therapy to bring additional medication to the dojo. She labels the bottles clearly and keeps them in the club's first aid box where they can be used when students forget to bring their regular supply.

Students can train virtually regardless of disability, with the sole exception of haemophilia. Regrettably jiu jitsu training can lead to haemorrhages which then require possible surgical intervention. Students with AIDS are not disqualified from training, provided that they cover all cuts and lesions with an occlusive dressing. The student is advised to consult his doctor where there is doubt about his health.

Having confirmed that the student is indeed fit to train, the next step is to locate a good jiu jitsu club. This is done by reading and acting upon the chapter of this book entitled 'Joining a good club'. It is one of the most important chapters in the whole book. By joining a good club, the student is automatically insured against loss of earnings resulting from training injury, or against being sued if he injures his partner. Though both of these situations are thankfully rare, they cannot be absolutely ruled out and a good insurance policy is no bad thing to have.

All equipment needed for training must be suitable for the purpose. New items should be bought only when they meet the required criteria for training. Old equipment should be checked to make sure it is safe and any defects remedied immediately. Some equipment may be unsafe for use and advice from the coach is required before a replacement is acquired. The club keeps a stock of the most commonly used items and generally these are cheaper than the equivalent items bought from sports shops.

If the student practises at home, then he must make sure there is a large enough space to practise in, and a soft enough floor to land on. Unmatted concrete floors are dangerous because of the possibility of falling awkwardly. A good thick carpet is the very least that can be used. The practice area must be cleared of obstacles such as chairs or tables, over which the student might trip. For obvious reasons, the student must keep away from any glass doors, radiators, or sharp edges (such as the corners of rooms).

The jiu jitsu training hall will be equipped with mats but the student must still take care not to get too close to the edge. Some clubs use mats which separate during practice. The student must keep an eye on these because many jiu jitsu injuries have resulted from getting a foot caught and twisted between them. During lulls in personal training, the student should sit with legs tucked up at the edge of the mat. Under no circumstances should he sprawl out, or lounge about. Training bags must be kept well away from the mat, and from access ways.

When several students are training together on a mat, a certain amount of observation is essential. The student must check that the coast is clear before attempting any throwing technique, because injuries have resulted from one student landing violently on top of another. One of the purposes of warm up exercise is to alert the mind to this possibility.

The student must always obey the directions of the coach. This is perhaps the cardinal rule of jiu jitsu practice. The command ''Stop!'' must be followed instantly. All activity must cease and attention is focussed on what is to be said or demonstrated.

Only the techniques shown may be practised and students must not under any circumstances attempt to introduce their own variations or interpretations. The training partner may be expected to perform a certain move that allows the defender to practise an arranged response but deviates from this because he wasn't told expressly what was required of him. This can and does result in injury. The problem is made worse if one partner is much larger (or much smaller). Large people generate a lot of power without realising it, and can cause injury with what is to them, a well controlled technique.

New techniques must be rehearsed slowly, and only when both participants are familiar with them, should the pace of practice increase. The execution of complex techniques is difficult at first, because the student is unused to the technique and each of its interlocking parts will have to be considered separately. It is only through constant repetition that the whole technique can be performed in one fast, flowing sequence.

Both partners must work at a mutually satisfactory speed – one that both can manage. Ideally, each student should work at near his maximum skill level for it is only when this is done that skill improves.

All attacking moves must be on target because if they are not, then the student learns only how to deal with an inaccurate technique. Some partners modify their response to suit the technique being practised. This is the kiss of death for skill acquisition. If the technique doesn't work, then the reason for failure must be discovered and remedied. Nothing is ever gained by 'going with the attack'.

If the attack is never violent, then the student learns only how to deal with a weak technique. At some stage, realism must be introduced!

Joining a Good Club

In some countries, the practice of martial art is accepted as a pastime which can have unfortunate spin-offs in terms of violence, crime, muggings etc. With this in mind, their governments have imposed laws which govern martial art practice for the safety of the public at large. There are no such laws in Great Britain, with the result that anyone can qualify themselves as a black belt 'expert' and start up a club.

As a reaction against this, the responsible members of Britain's martial art community enlisted the aid of the Sports Council, the Home Office and the Department of the Environment in setting up a recognised umbrella controlling body which would identify safe, competent martial art. That body is the Martial Arts Commission ('M.A.C.').

The Martial Arts Commission is the only martial arts organisation in membership of the prestigious Central Council for Physical Recreation. The M.A.C. also receives grant aid from the Sports council to assist its work in regulating and controlling martial art practice for the safety of the public. Could there be any better endorsement?

Though there are more than 120 individual schools of recognised martial art in Britain, each uses the M.A.C.'s distinctive logo and personal licence. There are many and various alternative certificates of competence to be had. Some are transcriptions of Chinese takeaway menus; others are issued by leading international martial art bodies. However, the only certificate which establishes beyond doubt the authenticity and standing of a club, is that issued by the Martial Arts Commission.

All members of the Martial Arts Commission subscribe to its Coaching Award Scheme. This is a code of training practice which ensures that not only are its certificated coaches highly skilled, but more importantly perhaps, they are competent to teach safely and effectively.

An additional good reason for only joining an M.A.C. recognised club is the insurance available to holders of commission licences. There are now over 100,000 licensed practitioners and this of course, represents very substantial purchasing power in terms of the scope of insurance coverage. Individual membership of the M.A.C. includes both a personal accident and public liability policy. These provide not only weekly and capital benefits in the unlikely event of injury, but they also indemnify students against claims arising if they injure other students.

All approved coaches hold a coaching indemnity insurance policy and this covers them against claims arising out of all accidents occurring during practice.

Individual governing bodies control the development of their own martial art within the Martial Arts Commission, and the body responsible for jiu jitsu is the British Jiu Jitsu Association ('B.J.J.A.'). the B.J.J.A. is solely responsible for the technical development of the art in Britain and any students wishing to affiliate should write, enclosing a stamped, addressed return envelope to:

The British Jiu Jitsu Association,
W.J.J.F.,
Barlows Lane,
Fazakerley,
Liverpool L9 9EH.

Glossary

Advanced level	A stage of sophisticated and effective practice which usually begins around brown belt level.
Ai	The Japanese term for 'harmony', used in martial arts to define the method by which the opponent's own force is turned and used against them.
Aikido	'The Way of All Harmony', a Japanese philosophy based upon the principles of aiki jitsu.
Aiki jitsu	'The Techniques of All Harmony', a school of traditional jiu jitsu founded during the period 1185-1382 by Shinra Saburo Yoshimitsu.
Aiki taiso	'Exercises of All Harmony', the basic exercises used in the practice of aikido.
Ankle lock	A technique which locks the ankle and causes pain.
Ankle throw	A sweeping technique in which the opponent is thrown with the foot or leg.
Arm lock	A technique which locks the elbow or shoulder, causing pain.
Art	Used in the martial arts sense, a skill or tradition of practice.
Ashi	The Japanese word for 'foot' or 'leg'.
Ashi ate	A set of kicking techniques taught in advanced jiu jitsu.
Ashi garami	'Leg entanglement', a lock which attacks and can dislocate the knee joint.
Ashi gatame	'Leg lock', an armlock which is applied by the leg.
Ashi guruma	'Leg wheel', a leg throw in which the student throws the opponent over his extended leg.
Ashi harai	'Leg sweeping', a trip in which the opponent's foot is displaced. Also known as 'ashi barai'.
Ashi hishigi	'Leg lock', a dislocation hold applied to the opponent's lower calf.
Ashikubi waza	'Ankle locking techniques', dislocation locks performed by forcing down, or twisting an opponent's foot.
Ashi sabaki	'Footwork', how the feet may be used.
Ashi waza	'Foot techniques', a collective name for all techniques using the foot or leg to throw the opponent.
Ate	'To strike', or 'striking'.
Atemi	'Body strikes', a method of attacking the body's pressure points.
Atemi waza	'The techniques of body strikes', also known as 'ate waza'.
Attention stance	A formal stance which the student adopts whilst awaiting a command.
Ayumi ashi	'Stepping foot', a method of keeping distance by alternately sliding the front and rear feet forwards or backwards.
Back fist	A strike made with the back of the knuckles.
Bajutsu	'The techniques of horsemanship', the way war horses were ridden in feudal Japan. Also known as 'jo-bajutsu'.
Ball of foot	The fleshy pad beneath the toes, used for kicking.
Basho	Grand sumo tournaments held annually in Japan.
Basics	The fundamental techniques of training.
Batto jutso	'Sword cutting technique', the art of drawing the sword and instantly using it. Similar to iai jutsu.
Belt	A cloth belt whose colour denotes the stage a student has reached in jiu jitsu practice.
Belt shoulder throw	A form of seoi nage, in which the ends of the belt rather than the jacket are used to throw the opponent.
Blocking	A technique which stops, hinders, or deflects an opponent's attack.
Bo	'Stave', a six foot staff used in bojutsu.
Body drop	A throwing technique in which the opponent is levered over an extended leg.
Bojutsu	'Stave techniques', the methods by which the staff is used as a weapon.
Bokken	'Wooden sword', a heavy wooden sword used both as a weapon and as a training aide.
Bow	To incline the head and upper body forward in a respectful greeting.
Breakfall	A method of falling safely by dispersing the force of landing.
Bu	'military', or 'martial'.

Budo	'Military way', systems of practice based upon martial art techniques but intended for self improvement.	Daisho	'Big and small', the two swords of the classical Japanese warrior.

Budo | 'Military way', systems of practice based upon martial art techniques but intended for self improvement.

Budoka | 'Person who follows the military way', a practitioner of budo.

Bugei | 'Martial arts', the name given to the practices of the traditional Japanese warrior.

Bugeisha | 'Person who practises martial arts', the formal name for an exponent of bugei.

Bujin | Same as bugeisha.

Bujutsu | 'Martial arts', a term similar to bugei.

Buke | 'Person of military rank', the samurai.

Bunkai | 'Analysis', the study and analysis of martial art techniques.

Bushi | 'Warrior', the name for the warrior class of Japan, of which the samurai were one rank.

Bushido | 'Way of the warrior', a code of behaviour observed by the bushi.

Choke | A hold which reduces or cuts off the supply of oxygenated blood to the brain.

Chudan | 'Middle level', the chest and stomach area.

Chunin | 'Middle person', an intermediate rank in ninjutsu.

Circular block | A method of deflecting an attack using a circular hand movement.

Collar shoulder throw | A form of seoi nage in which the thrower's arm is bent and placed under the opponent's armpit.

Collar wheel choke | A choke using the opponent's collar for purchase.

Combination | A series of techniques performed concurrently and/or consecutively.

Control | The regulation of force so that injury is avoided.

Coordination | The combination of distance, timing, speed, force and direction in such a way as to make the technique work.

Corner drop | A technique similar to kuki nage.

Corner throw | A sacrifice throw performed from prone position.

Counter attack | Retaliatory move made in response to an attack.

Cross chest choke | A technique which is a combination of a choke and a hold.

Dai sharin | 'Great wheel', a throwing technique developing a cartwheel-like movement.

Daisho | 'Big and small', the two swords of the classical Japanese warrior.

Daito | A long sword with cutting edge longer than 24".

Daito ryu | A classical martial art school.

Daki age | 'Hugging lift', a technique used during groundwork to lift the opponent.

Dakikomi jime | 'Hugging choke', a stranglehold.

Daki sutemi | 'Hugging sacrifice throw', a sacrifice technique normally used against a shorter opponent.

Dan | 'Position', a rank within the black belt such that:

1st dan	Shodan
2nd dan	Nidan
3rd dan	Sandan
4th dan	Yondan
5th dan	Godan
6th dan	Rokudan
7th dan	Shichidan
8th dan	Hachidan
9th dan	Kudan
10th dan	Judan

De ashi harai | 'Advancing foot sweep', the technique used to sweep opponent's foot.

Defence | A protective strategy or technique used in response to attack.

Defensive posture | A stance taken up in response to attack.

Deflect | To redirect.

Deshi | 'Disciple', or student.

Discipline | A form of training which develops character and physical ability.

Distraction | A move made to divert the opponent's attention.

Do | 'Way', a discipline or philosophy to follow.

Dogi | A training tunic.

Dojo | 'Place of training in the way', the training hall used for martial arts practice.

Dojo etiquette | The rules of good behaviour used in the martial art training hall.

Double handed neck lock | A double handed strangulation technique in which the carotid arteries are compressed.

Drop | A move which uses gravity to lower the body.

Ebi garami | 'Lobster entanglement', a form of strangulation technique.

Edge of foot	The edge of the foot between the base of the little toe and the heel, or between the base of the big toe and the heel. Used for kicking and sweeping respectively.
Edge of hand	That edge of the hand between the base of the little finger and the wrist, or between the base of the index finger and the wrist. Used for striking.
Elbow	Close quarter weapon or block.
Empi	Japanese word for elbow.
Eri seoi nage	'Lapel shoulder throw', a throw using the opponent's collar.
Finger locks	Locks applied to the joints of the fingers and thumb.
Fist	The area of the hand which includes the front of the knuckles.
Floating hip throw	A throw made with the hands.
floating hold	An immobilising hold.
Floating leg	The leg which is not supporting the weight of the body.
Focus	The maximum concentration of force at a particular instant.
Follow through	The continuation of a sequence to its conclusion.
Follow up	A technique which immediately follows another.
Foot throw	See 'ashi waza'.
Forearm	Area of the arm between elbow and wrist, used for blocking and striking.
Form	A type of practice consisting of predetermined techniques arranged into a pattern. Also known as 'kata'.
Form	The standard of technique presentation.
Fuki bari	'Needle blowing', a technique for spitting needles into an opponent's face. Used by the ninja.
Fukiya	Poison darts shot through a blowgun. Used extensively by the ninja.
Fukuro kensui	'Hanging bag', a form of necklock applied to the prone opponent.
Fundoshi	A traditional Japanese loin cloth.
Gake	The hooking ankle used in ankle and sacrifice throws.
Gaku	'Frame', the framed photograph of the founder of a ryu, or a philosophical text that is hung in traditional schools.
Ganseki otoshi	'Stone drop', a hand technique now rarely seen in training.
Garami	'Entanglement', a juxtaposition of arms or legs, so they locate against each other.
Gari	A reaping action performed by the foot.
Gasshuku	Training camp.
Gatame	'Locking', or 'holding', a way of immobolising the opponent.
Gedan	'Lower level', referring to the lower stomach, groin and upper thighs.
Gekigan jutsu	Techniques for utilising the ball and chain composite weapon.
Genin	Lowest rank of ninja.
Genkotsu	'Attacking vital points', a form of atemi waza.
Geta	Traditional Japanese wooden sandals.
Gi	'Tunic', the training uniform worn by martial artists.
Go no-sen	A successful counter attack which has exploited a failed attack.
Goshi	Japanese word for 'hip'.
Goshin jutsu	The techniques of self defence.
Grading	An examination of skill leading to promotion to a higher rank.
Grappling techniques	Techniques which use leverage rather than impact force.
Groundwork	Techniques performed when one or both participants are prone.
Guard	The position of the hands in relation to the stance.
Gyaku-	'Reverse', or 'opposite'.
Gyaku juji jime	'Reverse cross neck lock', a form of stranglehold.
Gyaku sankaku jime	'Reverse triangular neck lock', a form of stranglehold.
Gyaku te	'Reverse hand', the usage of locks and arm bars.
Gyaku tedori	'Reverse twisting', a wrist locking technique.
Gyaku yoko jujijime	'Side reverse cross necklock', a form of stranglehold.
Hachimaki	'Head wrapping', a cotton sweatband worn around the forehead.
Hadaka jime	'Naked necklock', a form of stranglehold.
Hairikata	Methods of entry into groundwork, or throwing techniques.
Hajime	'Begin', a Japanese command to commence training.
Hakama	'Split skirt', flowing trousers worn by the higher ranks.
Hakko ryu	A school of jiu jitsu which incorporates many atemi waza.
Halberd	An axe-like weapon with a long shaft.

Half side choke	A choke technique applied from the side.	Hiki-komi gaeshi	'Pulling in throw', a sacrifice throw performed from a prone position.
Hammer fist	The bottom of the clenched fist, used in a clubbing action.	Hiki otoshi	'Drawing drop'.
Hanbo	A stave used in bojutsu.	Hiki taotoshi	'Pull down', one of the elbow techniques mentioned above.
Hane goshi	'Springing hip throw', a hip throw which uses the hip and bent leg to lever the opponent over.	Hip rotation	Swivelling of the hips to generate power, or to withdraw the body.
Hane maki goshi	'Winding, springing hip throw', a type of sacrifice throw.	Hip throw	A throw made from standing position, and mainly using the hips for leverage.
Hane maki-komi	'Outer winding/springing hip throw'.	Hishigi hiza gatame	'Arm/knee lock', an armlock in which the knee is used to apply pressure to the elbow.
Hanging choke lock	A kneeling choke using both hands and the lower part of the leg.	Hiza	Japanese term for 'knee'.
Hanshi	Master grade of between 8th and 10th dan.	Hiza gatame	'Armlock with knee'.
Hara	'Stomach', the centre of the body's internal power. Situated near the navel.	Hiza gatame ude kukiji	'Knee/arm breaking', a lock which uses the knee to apply pressure to the arm.
Hara gatame	A form of arm bar which locks the opponent's arm against his stomach.	Hiza guruma	'Knee wheel', a leg technique in which the opponent is thrown in a wheel-like motion.
Hara gatame ude kujiki	An elbow lock using the stomach to apply force.	Hiza jime	'Choke lock with knee'.
Haragei	'Stomach arts', a way of concentrating internal power in the abdomen.	Hiza waza	'Knee techniques', the techniques of locking the knee joint.
Harai	'Sweep', as in foot sweep.	Hojo jutsu	'Techniques of tying', using a cord to immobilise the opponent.
Harai goshi	'Sweeping hip throw', a throw which lifts the opponent's forward thigh during its execution.	Ho jutsu	'The techniques of gunnery', the martial art of using firearms.
Harai maki-komi	'Sweeping, winding throw', a form of sacrifice throw.	Hold down	An immobilisation technique carried out on the ground.
Harai surikomi ashi	'Sweeping/drawing ankle throw', a form of foot sweep.	Honbu	'Headquarters', the centre for a martial art ryu.
Hara kiri	'Belly slitting', the informal term used to describe ritual suicide. See also 'seppuku'.	Hon gesa gatame	'Regular scarf hold', a hold down technique.
Hasamu	'To hold between', a way of holding the opponent between his legs during groundwork.	Iaido	'The way of sword drawing', a ritual based upon iaijutsu.
Heel of foot	Part of foot using during thrusting or stamping kicks.	Iaijutso	'The techniques of drawing the sword', the classical methods for drawing and using the sword.
Hidari	'Left'.	Idori	'Seated defence'.
Hiji	Japanese word for 'elbow'. See also 'empi'.	Instep	Part of the foot between the base of the toes and the front of the ankle, used in kicking techniques.
Hiji maki-komi	'Winding elbow lock', a holding technique used to immobilise the opponent.	Ippon seoi nage	'One arm shoulder throw', a throw in which the opponent is thrown over one shoulder.
Hiji otoshi	'Elbow drop', a technique using arm and hand movements to throw the opponent.	Jigo hontai	Defensive posture in which the feet are separated and the centre of gravity lowered by bending the knees.
Hiji waza	'Elbow techniques', a series of immobilising locks used to attack the elbow.	Jiu	'Gentle', or 'Yielding', the principle of giving way to an attacker's force and then immediately snapping back.

Jiu jitsu	'Techniques of yielding', an umbrella term for many traditional martial art ryu which taught techniques of striking, holding, locking and grappling.
Jo	'Stick', a short stick used in jo jutsu.
Jodan	'Upper part', the upper chest and head.
Jodo	'Way of the stick', a practice form based upon jo jutsu.
Jo jutsu	'Stick techniques', a fighting system using the jo.
Jonin	Ninja commander.
Judo	'The way of yielding', a combat sport based upon jiu jitsu.
Juji gatame	'Cross armlock', a straight arm lever applied across crossed legs.
Juji jime	'Cross lock', a choking technique in which both hands are used on opposite sides of the opponent's collar.
Jutsu	'Technique', the collection of practices which make up a martial art.
Jutte	A forked iron truncheon used by Japanese police.
Jutte jutsu	The techniques of using the jutte.
Kaeshi	The countering of an opponent's attack.
Kagi yari	'Key spear', a hooked spear used for hooking an opponent's weapon.
Kaiken	'Short knife', the dagger carried by all samurai women.
Kakato gaeshi	'Heel overturning', an unbalancing pull to the opponent's heel.
Kama	'Sickle', an agricultural implement used as a covert weapon.
Kamae	'Posture', the stance which a person adopts.
Kami uke gatame	Standing elbow lock.
Kancho	Headmaster of a martial art ryu.
Kangeiko	'Cold practice', a form of austere training in cold weather.
Kani basami	'Crab scissors', a throw which uses both legs in the manner of a crab's claws.
Kani waza	'Scissor technique', a throw in which the opponent's leg is scissored.
Kansetsu waza	'Locking techniques', the general term for all joint locking techniques.
Kasumi	'Mist', a feint used to disguise true intent.
Kata	See 'Form'.

Kata gatame	'Shoulder hold', the opponent is held by controlling his shoulders and one of his arms.
Kata guruma	'Shoulder wheel', a technique where the opponent is lifted onto the shoulders and then thrown down.
Kata hajime	'Single wing lock', a stranglehold used on a seated opponent.
Kata jujime	'Half cross neck lock', a hold performed with one hand while the opponent is prone.
Katana	'Sword', with a blade length of between 24"-36", worn cutting side upwards.
Kata oshi	'Shoulder push'.
Kata seoi	The single shoulder throw.
Katsugi jime	The shoulder neck lock.
Keibo	Wooden truncheon used by Japanese police.
Kendo	'Way of the sword', a combat sport based upon ken jutsu.
Ken jutsu	'Techniques of the sword', the way in which the Japanese warrior used his sword in combat.
Kesa gatame	'Scarf hold', a pinning technique.
Kesa gatame jime	'Cross chest stroke', a choke applied whilst in the scarf hold position.
Ki	'Spirit', the internal power within the body.
Kiai	'Spirit meeting', the unity of mind and body in performing a technique. Kiai is often expressed as a shout.
Knee	Part of the leg used in short distance strikes.
Knee locking techniques	Submission locks applied across the knee joint.
Knife hand	Open hand strike using the edge of the palm in a circular or thrusting motion.
Kobudo	'Way of weapons', a form of practice based upon the techniques for using traditional weaponry.
Kobu jutsu	'Weapon techniques', the method of using traditional weaponry in combat.
Kodachi	'Small sword', a sword with a blade length between 12"-18".
Kogusoku	A predecessor of jiu jitsu.
Kohai	A junior student.
Koshiguruma	A throw in which the opponent is grasped around the neck and thrown over the hip.
Koshi waza	'Hip techniques', those throwing techniques which involve the use of the hips.

Kosotogari	'Minor outer reaping', a throwing technique in which the opponent's leg is reaped from the outside.
Kote waza	'Wrist techniques', a series of wrist immobilisation techniques.
Ko uchi gake	The minor inner hooking throw.
Kuruma waza	'Wheel techniques', a series of throws in which the opponent's body travels through a wide arc before landing.
Kuzushi	'Upsetting', the method of disturbing the opponent's balance before attempting a technique.
Kyoshi	'Teaching grade', an instructor of 6th or 7th dan grade.
Kyu	'Grade', rank signified by a coloured belt.
Kyudo	'Way of the bow', a form of practice based upon kyu jutsu.
Kyu jutsu	'Techniques of Archery', the way in which the bow was used by the Japanese warrior during combat.
Kyu shin	The concept of using pliant postures and avoiding stiffness.
Leg throws	See 'ashi waza'.
Leg wheel	See 'ashi guruma'.
Leverage	A method of applying force, using a pivot, or 'fulcrum'.
Lock	A technique which immobilises a joint, or series of joints.
Maai	'Distancing', the distance between two opponents.
Mae sankaku jime	Front triangular choke.
Mae sumi otoshi	'Front corner drop', a hand throwing technique.
Mairi	Tapping with the hand on one's own body, or on the mat to signal that a technique has been properly applied.
Maki komi	'Winding', a turning movement of the body prior to certain throws.
Manriki gusari	'Ten thousand power chain', a length of chain with weighted ends.
Martial	Military or warlike.
Martial art	Military arts, arts of war.
Master	Title bestowed on a teacher after many years of accomplished study.
Ma sutemi waza	The collective name for throws practised from a prone position.
Meijin	'Expert', a title bestowed upon a person who has truly mastered a martial art.
Menkyo Kaiden	A certificate of proficiency issued by the master of a ryu to his successor.
Mizugumo	'Water wheel', a ninja device used for walking across water.
Mokuso	'Quiet thought', a form of meditation practised after training.
Morote gari	'Two handed reap', a throw to the rear executed by grasping an opponent's legs with two hands.
Morote jime	The two handed neck lock.
Morote seoi nage	The two handed shoulder throw.
Nage no kata	'Forms of throwing', a judo kata consisting of 15 throws.
Nage waza	'Throwing techniques', one of the three basic divisions of jiu jitsu practice.
Naginata	'Reaping sword', a halberd like weapon used for home defence, and as an anti-cavalry measure.
Naginata do	'The way of the reaping sword', a form of practice based upon naginata jutsu.
Naginata jutsu	'Techniques with the reaping sword', the usage of the naginata in a combat situation by the traditional Japanese warrior.
Nami juji jime	'Natural cross choke', a choke in which the arms are crossed and seize the opposite collar of the opponent's gi.
Neck lock	A method for immobilising the neck.
Ne waza	'Ground techniques', ground work.
Nihon seoi nage	'Two arm shoulder throw'.
Ninja	'Stealer in', a spy or assassin.
Ninjutsu	'Techniques of stealing in', the operational methods used by ninja.
Nunchaku	'Wooden flail', one of a group of Okinawan weapons now adopted by jiu jitsu.
Obi	'Belt'.
Obi otoshi	'Belt drop', a violent form of body drop.
Obi seoi	'Belt shoulder throw', a variation of seoi nage using the belt to lift the opponent.
Odachi	'Great sword', the longer sword of the daisho.
Ogoshi	'Major hip throw', a basic turning hip throw.
Oguruma	'Major wheel', a leg throw, using the extended feet.
Okuri ashi harai	'Sweeping ankle throw', the opponent's foot is swept as he is about to put weight onto it.
Osaekomi waza	'Methods of holding', the various types of holds.

O-sensei	'Great teacher', respectful title accorded to the chief instructor of a ryu.
Osoto gake	'Major outer dash', the opponent's leg is hooked and he is pushed backwards.
Osoto gari	'Major outer reap', the opponent is unbalanced to the rear as one of his legs is reaped.
Osoto guruma	'Major outer wheel', a throw in which both the feet are swept out.
Osoto maki-komi	'Major outer winding', a type of sacrifice throw.
Osoto otoshi	'Major outer drop', a leg throw in which the opponent is thrown backwards.
Otoshi	'Drop'.
Otsuri goshi	'Major lifting hip throw'.
Ouchi gari	'Major inner reap', a foot throw in which the opponent's foot is swept with a circular motion.
Palm-heel	The heel of the hand, used as a strike or block.
Pattern	A prearranged series of sequences of techniques. See also 'form' and 'kata'.
Pin	An immobilisation technique.
Posture	The stance used in relation to the technique being used.
Pressure points	Areas of the head, body and limbs which are susceptible to pressure.
Randori	'Free exercise', free association of techniques.
Randori waza	'Methods of free exercise', the techniques and strategies used during free exercise.
Rank	The level of proficiency held by a practitioner.
Reap	A leg action which sweeps away the foot/feet of an opponent.
Rei	A bow.
Renraku henka waza	'Combination techniques', a series of techniques where one leads logically into the next.
Renraku waza	'Continuation techniques', a diversionary attack followed by the main one.
Renshi	'Polished performer', a teacher of 5th-6th dan grade.
Reverse knife hand	A circular strike made with the thumb-edge of the palm. See 'ridge hand'.
Ridge hand	Another name for 'reverse knife hand'.

Rokushakubo	'Six foot staff' used in kobudo and kobujutsu.
Roll out	A method of dispersing the energy of a fall by converting the downward motion into a horizontal rolling motion.
Sacrifice throw	A system of throws in which both participants fall to the mat.
Sai	Okinawan threshing fork/truncheon adopted by jiu jitsu schools.
Sakasu juji jime	'Inverse cross neck lock'.
Samurai	'One who serves', name given to rank of Japanese warriors.
Sankaku	A triangular leg position used during groundwork.
Sankaku jime	'Triangular neck lock', a necklock in which the opponent's neck and one arm are locked.
Sasae surikomi ashi	'Propping/drawing ankle throw', the opponent is thrown with a lifting, sweeping motion.
Sasae surikomi ashi harai	'Propping/drawing ankle sweeping throw', a leg sweep technique.
Scissors	The legs are used to apply a hold.
Sekizui waza	'Methods of locking the spine', a class of dangerous jiu jitsu techniques.
Sempai	'Senior', title given to students of brown belt grade.
Sensen no-sen	The correct interpretation of the opponent's intentions.
Seoi hane goshi	'Shoulder spring hip throw'.
Seoi Maki-komi	'Winding shoulder throw', a hand technique.
Seoi nage	'Shoulder throw', a throw which takes the opponent over the shoulder.
Seppuku	The polite term for ritual suicide.
Shibori waza	'Methods of strangulation'.
Shihan	'Master teacher', an award conferred upon instructors of above 6th dan.
Shiho gatame kei	'Four quarters locking system', the generic name for a group of holding techniques.
Shime waza	'Methods of strangulation', a collective name for those locks which cut off the supply of oxygenated blood to the brain.
Shinai	A bamboo practice sword.
Shinobi shozoku	A form of uniform worn by the ninja.
Shochu geiko	Traditional training period lasting for up to 30 days held during the hottest time of the year.
Shoshinsha	'Novice', any ungraded practitioner.

Shugyosha	Person who is undergoing intense training.
Shugyo	'Training', especially hard training.
Shuko	Type of knuckleduster used by the ninja.
Shuriken	Ninja throwing stars.
Side kick	A kick which travels out sideways from the body and contacts with the outer edge of the foot.
Sode uguruma	'Sleeve wheel'.
Sode guruma jime	'Lapel wheel choke'.
Sode surikomi goshi	'Sleeve lifting hip throw', both the opponent's sleeves are grasped and he is pulled up and over the hip.
So jutsu	'Spear techniques', the methods of using a spear in combat.
Soto maki-komi	'Outer winding throw', a form of sacrifice throw.
Staff	A wooden stave about six feet in length.
Stamping kick	A thrust kick directed downwards and contacting with the heel.
Stance	The position of hands and feet in relation to a technique.
Stave	See 'staff'.
Stomach throw	The opponent is thrown in a roll back action. See also 'tomoe nage'.
Striking techniques	Techniques which develop their effect through impact.
Style	A form of martial art practice reflecting the interpretation of the founder.
Suiei jutsu	'Swimming techniques', the ways of swimming silently etc, for military purposes.
Sukui	To scoop up.
Sukui nage	'Scooping throw', the opponent is lifted up, turned and dropped onto his back.
Sumo	Japanese wrestling.
Sutemi	'Sacrifice'.
Sutemi waza	'Methods of sacrifice', forms of throwing in which both participants fall to the mat.
Sweep	A method of disturbing the opponent's balance by using the legs to move one or both of his feet.
Tachi	Japanese longsword worn with the cutting edge downwards and used from horseback.
Tachi waza	'Standing methods', a collective name for techniques performed from a standing position.

Taiho jutso	'Arrest techniques', techniques used by the police.
Tai jutsu	'Body art', one of the predecessors of jiu jitsu.
Tai otoshi	'Body drop', the opponent is thrown back over an extended leg.
Tai sabaki	'Body movement', the turning action of the body required to perform certain throws.
Takedown	A technique which takes the opponent down to the mat.
Tanbo	'Short stick'.
Tanden	'Abdomen', the body's centre of gravity.
Tanto	A Japanese dagger with a blade 8"-16" long.
Tanto jutsu	'Knife techniques', the ways in which the knife is used during combat.
Tatami	Straw mat measuring three feet by six feet, by three inches thick.
Tate shiho gatame	'Vertical four corner holding', a hold down technique in which the opponent is straddled and both arms are wrapped around his neck.
Tawarra gaeshi	A form of sacrifice throw.
Teguruma	'Hand wheel', a counter attack used against a poorly executed sweeping hip throw or similar.
Tenshin shinyo ryu	An early style of jiu jitsu.
Tessen jutsu	Techniques for using the iron fan as a method of self defence.
Tetsubo	'Iron staff', a heavy metal staff.
Te waza	'Hand methods', a collective term used to describe standing throws performed by hand and arm movements.
Tobi goshi	'Jumping hip throw', a counterattack to most hip throws.
Tokushi keibo	A telescopic truncheon.
Tomoe nage	See 'stomach throw'.
Tonfa	An Okinawan covert weapon now adopted by jiu jitsu.
Tori te	'Taking hands', a predecessor of jiu jitsu.
Toshu kakuto	System of unarmed combat devised for Japanese armed forces.
Tsubame gaeshi	'Swallow counter', defence against a hip throw.
Tsukuri	Breaking the opponent's balance by a combination of arms and body action.
Uchi deshi	'Apprentice', where the student was apprenticed to a martial art master.

Uchi maki-komi	'Inner winding throw', a type of sacrifice throw.	Wakizashi	Short sword with blade length of 16"-23".
Uchi mata	'Inner thigh throw', a throw performed by sweeping the leg up and between the opponent's.	Waza	'Method'.
		Wrist lock	The application of pressure across the wrist joint.
Ude garami	'Entangled armlock', the opponent's arm is bent and pressure applied to his elbow.	Yamei	'Halt!', Japanese command to stop.
		Yoi	'Prepare!', Japanese command to make ready to practise.
Ude gatame	The opponent's elbow is locked.	Yoko gake	'Side body drop', a type of side sacrifice technique.
Ude hishigi	The straight arm locks.		
Ude waza	The collective name for techniques applied against the elbow joint.	Yoko guruma	'Side wheel', a counter used against hip throw.
Uke	The partner on whom the technique is executed.	Yoko jime	'Cross side choke', a stranglehold applied as the opponent attempts to rise.
Ukemi	'Art of falling', the methods by which the energy of the falling body are dispersed.	Yoko maki-komi	'Side winding throw', a throwing technique.
Ura nage	'Rear throw', a type of sacrifice throw.	Yoko otoshi	'Side drop', a type of sacrifice technique.
Ura waza	'Methods of reversing a technique', where the opponent's response is anticipated and successfully countered.	Yubi jutsu	The techniques of using the thumb and fingers to attack the vital points.
		Yudansha	Holder of black belt.
Ushiro goshi	'Rear hip throw', a form of counter attack.	Zen	Form of Buddhism favoured by traditional warriors because of its belief in self-reliance.
Utsuri goshi	'Changing hip throw', a form of counter attack to hip throws.		
Vital points	Areas of the body which, when struck, can result in injury, or even death.		

Index